A FAMILY GUIDE TO
TERRARIUMS
for Kids

Inspiring | Educating | Creating | Entertaining

Brimming with creative inspiration, how-to projects, and useful information to enrich your everyday life, Quarto Knows is a favorite destination for those pursuing their interests and passions. Visit our site and dig deeper with our books into your area of interest: Quarto Creates, Quarto Cooks, Quarto Homes, Quarto Lives, Quarto Drives, Quarto Explores, Quarto Gifts, or Quarto Kids.

First Published in 2020 by Cool Springs Press, an imprint of The Quarto Group, 100 Cummings Center, Suite 265-D, Beverly, MA 01915, USA.
T (978) 282-9590 F (978) 283-2742 QuartoKnows.com

Cool Springs Press titles are also available at discount for retail, wholesale, promotional, and bulk purchase. For details, contact the Special Sales Manager by email at specialsales@quarto.com or by mail at The Quarto Group, Attn: Special Sales Manager, 100 Cummings Center, Suite 265-D, Beverly, MA 01915, USA.

24 23 22 21 20   2 3 4 5

ISBN: 978-0-7603-6734-6

Digital edition published in 2020

eISBN: 978-0-7603-6735-3

Library of Congress Cataloging-in-Publication Data

Names: Buzo, Patricia, author.

Title: A Family guide to terrariums for kids : imagination-inspiring projects to grow a world in glass / Patricia Buzo.

Description: Beverly, MA : Cool Springs Press, 2020. | Includes index. |

Audience: Ages 4 to 12 | Summary: "With Terrariums for kids, budding botanists and artists can build, plant, and grow their own living worlds under glass following 15 unique and inspiring terrarium plans"-- Provided by publisher.

Identifiers: LCCN 2020012691 | ISBN 9780760367346 (trade paperback) | ISBN 9780760367353 (ebook)

Subjects: LCSH: Terrariums--Juvenile literature. | Glass gardens--Juvenile literature.

Classification: LCC SB417 .B89 2020 | DDC 635.9/824--dc23

LC record available at https://lccn.loc.gov/2020012691

Design & Page Layout: Mattie Wells

Photography: Tracy Walsh

Printed in China

A FAMILY GUIDE TO
TERRARIUMS
for Kids

Imagination-inspiring Projects to Grow a World in Glass

PATRICIA BUZO

COOL SPRINGS PRESS

Contents

Introduction (7)

SECTION 1: PARTS OF A TERRARIUM (8)

SECTION 2: TERRARIUM PROJECTS FOR KIDS (52)

INTRODUCTION

As a child, I loved to help work in my mom's garden, that is until a found a slimy grub worm while digging in the soil! Eeek! That turned me off playing in the dirt for a while. Thankfully, it wasn't long before my love of gardening and plants returned, and after all these years I still like to get my hands dirty!

A love of caring for plants is, to me, a fundamental part of growing up. Kids who learn to care for nature grow up to be adults who care for nature. This book was written with the intention not only of educating kids about terrariums, but also nurturing a curiosity for all things living, whether they be tiny plants or tiny animals.

We will be discussing each element in making terrariums with a variety of plant types and how to care for them. Which plants belong in an open container and which in a sealed jar? What plants grow well together? How do you maintain a terrarium? What is a bioactive terrarium and why is it important? All these questions and more are covered in this in-depth yet easy-to-understand manual.

Finally, there are 15 fun and exciting step-by-step terrarium projects introducing a variety of plant groups that both kids and adults can enjoy creating. Moss, succulents, cacti, aquatic plants, mini trees, and even living rocks, all are fascinating plants with unique requirements that are featured throughout the book. I encourage making time to work on these projects as a family; it will be time together you can look back on fondly for many years to come. Alternatively, a classroom terrarium project will not only be a quality educational experience but lots of fun too.

Making terrariums begins with learning the basic parts of a terrarium. So let's get started!

PICKING THE RIGHT CONTAINER

The container you choose for your plants will contribute to the long-term success of your terrarium. There are many styles to choose from: tall or short, round or square, lid or no lid. Before you choose your container consider the types of plants you want to use. The type of container you pick will depend on the plants' needs.

PLACES TO FIND TERRARIUM CONTAINERS

Shopping for a container is half the fun of making your new terrarium! You can find them for sale at secondhand stores, craft stores, and big box stores. You can also recycle canning jars, vases, and fishbowls to use as terrarium containers.

Choosing the Right Container for Your Terrarium

Lid or No Lid

If you want to use tropical plants, mosses, or ferns in your terrarium, I recommend choosing a container with a lid. These types of plants love humidity, and a container that can be sealed with a lid is a great way to trap moisture inside. However, if you plan on planting succulents, cacti, or air plants, it's best to pick a lidless container with a large opening so that your plants will have lots of airflow. Open containers are also best for plants that like lots of sun because if they were to be planted in a covered container, the Sun's intense rays could "cook" the plants inside and kill them.

What Kind of Material Should It Be Made Of?

When choosing a container, you will have a few options of what they are made of. Clear glass is the most common and is readily available. You may even find tinted glass containers that are a transparent green or blue color. There is nothing wrong with using lightly tinted glass, but keep in mind that the tint will reduce the amount of light that enters the jar so you will have to choose plants accordingly. Another good option is acrylic (a type of plastic). Acrylic containers are nice because they are less likely to break and have no sharp edges. These containers may be more suitable for younger kids or very accident-prone people (I speak from experience). The downside of acrylic containers is they scratch easily.

The Shape of the Container

Glass containers come in many shapes so you can pick the look you like. Just remember that if the jar has a very small opening it will be more difficult to get your plants inside. To begin, I recommend starting with a container into which you can fit your hand. Also important is the size. If you have chosen plants that potentially grow very large over time, then perhaps choose a large vase so that the plant has lots of room to grow upwards. A fishbowl is an ideal container for a wide variety of tropical plants as well as being suitable for moss. The globe shape will trap some moisture inside, but a lid should also be used for mosses and other humidity-loving plants. I sometimes use a glass plate as a lid if the bowl didn't come with one. You could also cover it with plastic wrap and cut away the excess around the rim. Plants such as cacti, air plants, and succulents do best when they are planted in glass half-bowls (these have a shape more like a cereal bowl than a fishbowl) or hanging globes with a large opening for airflow.

Types of Containers

Canning Jars: a canning jar is a great home for moss because it is small in size and also has a lid to keep moisture locked inside.

Vases: tall, open-top vases work very well for plants that grow to be very tall or trail, such as vining plants. Tall jars and vases are also very well suited for Lady Slipper Orchids.

Fishbowls and Half-bowls: with or without a lid, fishbowls make wonderful homes for a wide variety of plants. Some suggestions are moss, Peperomias, and small ferns. The bigger the bowl, the more plants you can fit. Half-bowls are the only type of containers I recommend for planting cacti and succulents. They are shaped to allow a lot of airflow and can be placed in direct sunlight without harming the plant.

Bell Jars: as the name suggests, these jars are in the shape of a bell and are placed over a potted plant to trap in moisture. I suggest using ferns, some carnivorous plants, bonsai, and tropical foliage plants for bell jars.

Cookie Jars: glass cookie jars are perfect for humidity-loving plants like mosses and ferns, as well as tropical foliage plants. These containers are like canning jars but give you more space to work with.

Hanging Containers: hanging containers come in many shapes and sizes. These are perfect for air plants and some smaller varieties of succulents to live in.

Candy Jars: these can be used for any type of humidity-loving plant such as moss, small ferns, and tropical foliage plants.

PREPARING YOUR CONTAINER FOR PLANTING

In order to prepare your new terrarium, it's important to choose the right growing medium for your plants. It can make the difference between a successful terrarium with lush plant growth or dead plants! In this chapter I will discuss the different substrate options and when and how to use them. We will also talk a little about decorative elements that you can add to personalize your terrarium.

Growing Mixes

All-purpose Potting Soil: Usually an all-purpose potting soil made for houseplants consists of a blend of peat moss, humus, and perlite. Sometimes fertilizers are added directly to the mix. This type of soil is excellent for tropical plants and ferns because it retains a lot of moisture. You will normally use this type of soil over a layer of gravel and/or horticultural charcoal so that there is enough drainage and the plants' roots don't rot from too much water staying in the soil. If you want a bit more aeration you can add extra perlite.

Perlite: Perlite is a hard, porous material made by superheating volcanic glass, which makes it an excellent soil additive when you have a plant that likes more aerated soil. Normally it's not used on its own as a substrate because it does not retain water and has none of the beneficial elements for plants found in soil.

Cactus and Succulent Mix: These mixes are made of natural substances that are fast-draining like pumice, bark, and sand. Research the plants you will be using before choosing a brand of succulent or cactus mix. Some plants like a sandier soil while others prefer something a little different. Usually cacti prefer a sandier mix than succulents do but not always, so again, do your research by looking online about your specific plants.

Coco Coir: Coco coir is made of ground up coconut shells and is an inert substrate, meaning it doesn't have nutrients in it. It's perfect for plants like moss that have no root systems or plants that are very sensitive to rich soils. As an added benefit, I've noticed mold is less likely to hitch a ride on coco coir than it is on soil, and mold can be a major problem in terrariums. So this substrate combined with springtails (see chapter 4) keep mold away from my moss! Coco coir can also be added to other mixes and has a few other key benefits: it holds up to ten times its weight in water, it does not decompose as rapidly as peat moss, and it is friendlier to the environment.

Carnivorous Soil Mix: Carnivorous plants vary in their needs but most of them prefer a soil that retains a lot of moisture but allows air circulation in the soil. A good all-purpose carnivorous mix is made up of about two-thirds organic peat moss and one-third vermiculite and/or perlite. Alternatively a mix of two-thirds peat moss and one-third sand is also good. Many carnivorous plants can also live in plain, 100 percent long fiber sphagnum moss. Because most come from nutrient-poor soils and have become carnivorous to absorb nutrients through the insects they catch. Sphagnum moss, when used as a substrate, needs to be replaced every year. However, repotting with sphagnum is a breeze, so it's still a good choice for many carnivorous plants.

Bonsai Mix: The bonsai mix you choose will depend on the type of tree you are using. Certain tree types will require more moisture than others, such as the Brazilian Raintree discussed in chapter 3; for these, you can use a substrate with some peat moss or coco coir in it. But other types, such as the Ginseng Ficus (see page 38), are not quite as picky and can be planted in an all-purpose bonsai mix.

Orchid Mix: The mix you choose will depend on the type of orchid you are planting. Most prefer a well-aerated mix that still retains moisture. Many orchids do well in LECA clay balls or pure sphagnum moss. But another option is to use an all-purpose orchid mix, which is usually made up of fir bark and perlite.

LECA: LECA stands for "lightweight expanded clay aggregate" and is made by heating clay at very high temperatures and tumbling it until it puffs into little balls. It's very good for growing many types of orchids and when growing plant cuttings, as discussed in chapter 4. It contains no nutrients for plants to use as food so some sort of fertilizing will be necessary; I prefer using a foliar spray or slow-release pellets especially for orchids.

Long Fiber Sphagnum Moss: For many plants, such as certain orchids and carnivorous plants, pure, long fiber sphagnum moss is an excellent choice. It does a very good job of retaining moisture but is very low in nutrients, which is what these plants are used to in the wild. Using sphagnum is easy; dampen it in distilled water, squeeze it out like a sponge, and wrap up the roots of the plant.

Horticultural Charcoal: Though charcoal isn't used as a mix by itself, it is a beneficial additive to many soil mixes because it adds aeration, and freshens and purifies the mix. I like to use it as a drainage layer, which has the added benefit of keeping things smelling fresh.

MIXES FOR AQUATIC PLANTS

Planting mixes for aquariums or paludariums can be anything from sand, gravel, and small rocks to specialized mixes such as Eco-Complete by Caribsea. Whatever you choose, rinse it before adding it to your container (unless otherwise specified on the package) to avoid cloudy water.

Decorative Elements

Many things can be used to spruce up the look of your terrarium. Here is a short list of suggested decorative elements to personalize your terrarium creation:

- ▶ Brightly colored sand or aquarium gravel
- ▶ River rock
- ▶ Sea glass
- ▶ Marbles
- ▶ Glitter
- ▶ Crushed glass without sharp edges (from craft stores)

- Crystals and geodes
- Seashells
- Driftwood
- Fossils
- Fairy garden miniatures
- Toy animal figures
- Railroad miniatures (HO, G, and O scale)

Note: Try to stay away from things such as pinecones, branches from the outside, or other natural elements in closed jars. These are mold and fungus magnets and can cause a lot of trouble in a sealed, humid environment. It's best to choose non-organic decorations made of rock, glass, or plastic instead.

THE BEST PLANTS FOR TERRARIUMS

Making a terrarium starts with planning and choosing the types of plants you want to keep. The good news is there are lots of plant options from which to choose. Many of these grow well together in the same container. Making a plant list is a great way to start. Using a piece of paper and the plant lists in this chapter, write the name of the plant you would like to use in one column; in another column, write the conditions that plant likes to live in. Is it a plant that needs to stay dry or does it need a lot of moisture and humidity? Does it like lots of sunlight or does it prefer shade?

You will notice that some of the plants on your list like to live in the same conditions and will therefore grow well together. Once you have completed your list, you can get started by purchasing the plants and materials you will need. The following pages feature some of my favorite plant groups to use in terrariums.

Magnificent Moss

Moss is an excellent choice for covered terrariums because it loves humidity. Unlike most plants, moss does not have any roots. Instead, it anchors itself to a variety of surfaces using rhizoids. The sole purpose of the rhizoids is to help the moss hold on tightly. That means moss absorbs all the nutrients and moisture it needs through its leaves. You can either purchase moss for your terrarium from a supplier or go moss hunting in the woods.

Moss Care

Moss should be kept in a terrarium with a lid so that its leaves can stay hydrated in a humid environment. (Remember: moss cannot drink water through its roots because it doesn't have any.) You should spray your terrarium once every 2 to 3 months, enough to dampen the surface of the moss. It's important to use distilled water, which can be purchased at a grocery store, because moss is sensitive to the additives in tap water. Once or twice a year, you can pour in a small amount of water to keep the soil moist, which will also help raise the humidity inside the sealed jar. Place your moss terrarium in a location that is in bright, but not direct, sunlight.

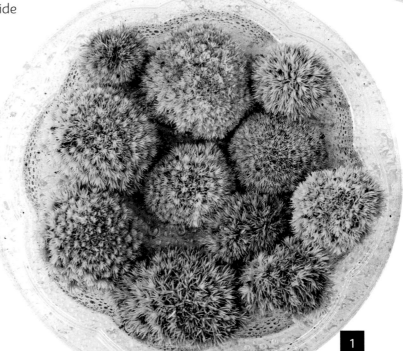

1

There are several types of moss that do especially well in terrariums, such as:

1. Cushion Moss (*Leucobryum*): Cushion Moss grows in small clumps that look like tiny green pillows. It is low-growing and can be placed at the front of the terrarium to look like grassy hills.

2. Rock Cap Moss (*Dicranum*): Rock Cap Moss is bushy, grows taller than Cushion Moss, and is darker green in color. These features make it an ideal plant for the back of the terrarium to simulate trees in the distance.

3. Fern or Feather Moss (*Hypnum* or *Ptilium*): Fern and Feather Mosses look just like miniature fern fronds and range in color from light green to reddish brown. It grows in a dense mat, which is why it is also sometimes called Sheet Moss. The individual pieces can be pulled from the mat and used to accent your tiny landscapes.

GO ON A MOSS HUNT

Moss hunting is fun! Find a wooded area with lots of shade. Make sure you have permission to collect moss at the location you choose. You can find moss growing on the ground or on the sides of rocks and trees.

What you will need: plastic baggies, a spoon, and gloves (optional). With your spoon, gently shovel up pieces of moss from the surfaces on which they're growing. Place the pieces in a plastic bag, and seal. Moss can be stored in the refrigerator inside the plastic baggies for a few weeks.

Sensational Succulents and Cacti

The word "succulent" simply means that a plant has plump, fleshy leaves that store water. Succulents and cacti can make great candidates for terrariums as long as their specific needs are met. Whether they have spines or are smooth, all are considered succulents. They come from places that may not get a lot of rainfall, so they need to conserve the water they get for long periods of time. This means that when they're kept as houseplants, and especially in a terrarium, you don't want to accidentally overwater them. This could cause them to rot, especially since there's no hole in the bottom of a terrarium pot for extra water to drain out.

Succulent and Cacti Care

The soil mix used for cacti and succulents has excellent drainage, and normally consists of sand, small gravel, bark chips, and perlite. Extra care must be taken to be very sure you don't water too much. Succulents can handle drought much better than they can handle excess water. You can tell if your plant is thirsty by looking to see if the bottom leaves have become dry and crispy while the top of the plant still looks normal. However, since old leaves (the ones at the bottom) naturally dry as the plant grows, this isn't a fool-proof method.

Succulent plants and cacti generally need a lot of light, which equates to several hours of direct sunlight per day. In the case of succulents, you may be able to get away with no direct sunlight as long as the location is as brightly lit as possible, such as an east- or west-facing windowsill. Cacti, on the other hand, require several hours of sun exposure every day. Ideally try to place your succulent/cactus terrarium near a bright window, or, if a bright location isn't available, under grow lights. Keep in mind that glass magnifies the Sun's rays and heat. Never plant succulents or cacti in a covered glass terrarium or one with very tall sides. The containers should always be an open-style half-bowl or something similar.

SOME OF MY FAVORITE SUCCULENTS AND CACTI

My favorite succulents are:

- Living Stones (*Lithops*)
- String of Pearls (*Senecio rowleyanus*)
- Echeveria rosettes (*Haworthia cooperi*)
- Fasciated Haworthia (*Haworthiopsis fasciata*)

My favorite cacti are:

- Bunny Ears (*Opuntia microdasys*)
- Sea Urchin Cactus (*Astrophytum asterias*)
- Fire Sticks (*Euphorbia tirucalli*)

Lithops are succulent plants called "Living Stones" because they resemble rocks on the ground.

Amazing Air Plants

Air plants make wonderful low-maintenance terrarium inhabitants. The scientific name for air plant is *Tillandsia*. They are a unique type of plant because they don't grow in the ground and don't have traditional roots like other plants do. They are "epiphytes," meaning they grow clinging to other surfaces like tree branches. A few other plants grow this way, too, such as Bromeliads and certain types of orchids. All these kinds of plants receive most of the nutrients they need by absorbing them from the air as they are soaking up moisture through their leaves when it rains. Generally, air plants like to live in a more humid environment so their leaves don't dry out and get crispy. However, that doesn't necessarily mean they like to live in a closed terrarium. Most of the time closed terrariums stay too wet for air plants because they like to dry out in between watering. Also, if the base of the plant is kept wet even for just a day, it will likely start to rot and die. For these reasons I recommend using a terrarium container with an opening. Hanging glass orbs make an excellent choice, as do open vases.

Air Plant Care

Tillandsias like bright but indirect light. A good location is somewhere close to a window that doesn't receive direct sunlight. If your bathroom has a window, that is great place to put them because it will be more humid in the bathroom than other rooms of the house.

Many people like to soak their air plants in water for around 15 to 30 minutes and then leave them out to dry. I have found that this method is tricky when keeping air plants indoors. Often the base of the plant doesn't dry out thoroughly enough, even after several hours, and they rot. Instead, I prefer to mist my air plants with distilled water every week. I spray them enough to change the color of their leaves, but I avoid letting water collect in the centers of the plants. Then I let them sit out for a few hours to dry and place them back in the terrarium. A general rule of thumb is the fuzzier the air plant, the less water it will require. By "fuzzy," I mean plants whose leaves have tiny hairs on them; these hairs are usually whitish. Air plants with no fuzz dry out very quickly and prefer a more humid environment to stay healthy.

TILLANDSIAS

Tillandsias bloom when they are mature, and the flowers are usually very brightly colored. You can tell they are about to bloom because, in many varieties, the leaves will blush, or turn pink, right beforehand. They only bloom once in their lifetime but something exciting happens soon after they flower: at the base of the plant, tiny babies, called "pups," will begin to grow. These pups continue to grow over the next several months and eventually will also flower. You can leave them attached to the mother plant and have a cluster of air plants or remove the pups when they are at least half the size of the mother plant. To give these growing plants a boost you can use a fertilizer made specially for *Tillandsia* at half the recommended strength. A little goes a long way, so don't overdo it with fertilizers.

NEOREGELIA AND CRYPTANTHUS BROMELIADS

These two types of Bromeliads can also be used in terrariums and vivariums. They are like Tillandsias in that they receive much of the nutrients and moisture they require through their leaves. But unlike air plants, Neoregelias like to have water sitting in the center "cup" of their leaves. They grow more traditional roots than do air plants. They prefer their roots to be kept moist at all times, so planting Neoregelias in long fiber sphagnum moss or a well-aerated potting mix is acceptable. Cryptanthus are also Bromeliads, but they are terrestrial plants and have roots in the truest sense of the word. They should be planted in a peat-based potting mix that is kept moist. Besides these few differences they have many of the same needs that air plants have: bright indirect light, humid environment preferred, water by misting with distilled water, and use diluted foliar fertilizer.

Fabulous Ferns

If there ever were a perfect terrarium plant, it would be the fern! There are thousands of different types of ferns. In nature, ferns grow in shady, humid conditions like the forest floor. Of course, not every type will be suitable for terrarium life, but many smaller varieties do very well under glass. Ferns pair well with other tropical plants and moss; feel free to mix and match!

Fern Care

Truthfully, most fern species don't stay small, so it is best either to choose a large terrarium to begin with or, if a smaller one is used, plan on lots of pruning and eventually replanting it in a larger container. (A large container is anything over 12 inches [30.5 cm] wide and high.)

Ferns love humidity and damp soil, but that doesn't mean they like their feet sopping wet. They can rot just like any other terrestrial plant that sits in standing water for too long. Damp or moist soil is about the same consistency as a dish sponge that you wring out; it's wet but not dripping. Creating drainage in your terrarium is a good idea so that if you accidentally water a little too much it can drain to the bottom and not cause harm to plant roots. I usually start with a few inches (5 cm) of gravel or horticultural charcoal at the bottom of the container for this purpose.

You have a choice whether to cover a fern terrarium or not. If the opening is only a few inches (5 cm), then you don't need to cover it because enough moisture will still get trapped inside. However, if your container has a very wide opening you may want to consider covering it. Uncovered terrariums will need to be watered more often than covered ones.

A FEW OF MY FAVORITE FERNS

- Cretan Brake Fern (*Pteris cretica*)
- Spider Fern (*Arachnoides simplicior*)
- Blue Star Fern (*Phlebodium aureum*)
- Lemon Button Fern (*Nephrolepis cordifolia* 'Duffii')
- Spike Moss (*Selaginella*), which is not really a moss but is closely related to ferns (called a "fern ally").
- Another plant that does well in larger terrariums is Asparagus Fern (*Asparagus setaceus*), although it is not a true fern.

Cool Creeping Plants

Vining plants that creep along on long stems and eventually cover a surface are a good choice for terrariums but will most likely need frequent haircuts. Luckily many of them also can be propagated (make new plants) from the clippings. You can allow these plants to cover the bottom of the terrarium or give them things to climb on like large stones. Some of them can smother other slow-growing plants, which will keep them from getting the light they need, so make sure you prune them if they start to get out of control.

Creeping Plant Care

Since there are many different plants that creep, the care of each one depends on that particular plant. I encourage you to look at the amount of light your room gets and then choose a creeping plant that would do best in that light level. Be sure to adjust how often you water the plants to their favorite conditions.

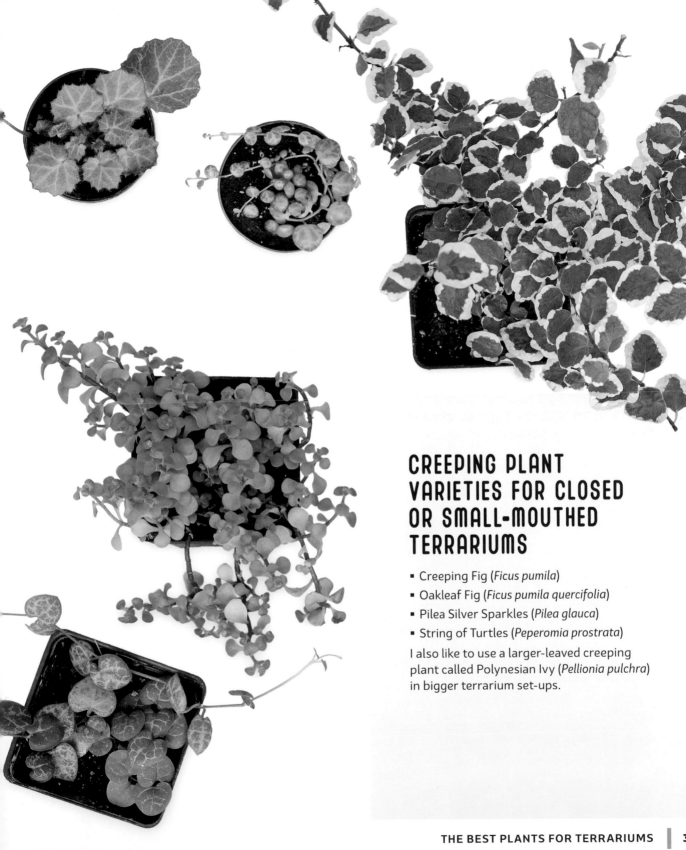

CREEPING PLANT VARIETIES FOR CLOSED OR SMALL-MOUTHED TERRARIUMS

- Creeping Fig (*Ficus pumila*)
- Oakleaf Fig (*Ficus pumila quercifolia*)
- Pilea Silver Sparkles (*Pilea glauca*)
- String of Turtles (*Peperomia prostrata*)

I also like to use a larger-leaved creeping plant called Polynesian Ivy (*Pellionia pulchra*) in bigger terrarium set-ups.

Captivating Carnivorous— "Meat-eating"—Plants

No, they don't really eat meat like we do. In fact, giving your carnivorous plant a piece of hamburger would do more harm than good. But they do appreciate living food (bugs!) from time to time. Carnivorous plants, or CPs, grow in very nutrient-poor soils in the wild, so they have adapted to absorb the nutrients they need by eating insects. There are certainly many types of carnivorous plants out there, but only a few are suitable for life in a terrarium.

Carnivorous Plant Care

All carnivorous plants must be watered with mineral-free distilled water, including all those discussed in this section, as tap water has additives that will slowly kill these plants. If your CP has hollow leaves, make sure they are always filled halfway with liquid and, if needed, add some distilled water to them with a small syringe. See the following plant descriptions to learn more about caring for each type.

HOW DO CPs CATCH BUGS?

One way that CPs catch their prey is by producing dew, nectar, and other sticky stuff that insects find irresistible. Unfortunately for the insect, once it lands on the plant, it gets stuck and dies. The plant then absorbs the bug's juices just like fertilizer. (Gross or cool? You decide!)

Another way CPs catch insects is by tricking them by setting traps. Some CPs have leaves that form tall cups that fill with rainwater. At the top there may be nectar, and when a bug crawls on the slippery surface, it falls into the cup below only to drown and then be absorbed by the plant.

Some plants have developed a kind of spring trap with tiny hairs on the surface. When the insect triggers a few of those hairs, the trap springs closed and captures its prey!

JUST SAY NO TO VENUS FLY TRAPS

Most people have heard of the Venus Fly Trap (VFT), with its leaves that look like mini spring traps. They are supercool plants. You may be wondering why I don't recommend them for terrariums. First, VFTs need lots of direct sunlight, at least 6 hours per day if not more. That's hard to replicate indoors, even in a sunny window. Second, all VFTs need to go through a long rest period during the winter, at least 3 to 5 months. During that time, pretty much all their leaves turn brown, shrivel, and die. They still need light, but not heat, which is another thing that is difficult to achieve inside of a house. Then, to bring a VFT out of this rest period, you must gradually raise the temperature and hours of light the plant gets until it starts to grow again. For all these reasons, I don't recommend them as good terrarium occupants.

Favorite Easy-care CPs

Sundew

Sundew (*Drosera*) have leaves that either look like octopus tentacles with droplets of nectar that act like glue for an insect that lands on them, like *D. capensis*, or they can look like a flower with many sticky petals, like *D. spatulata*. They prefer poor-quality soil (meaning, no added fertilizers) that remains wet all the time. In nature, Sundew plants tend to grow near water, sometimes even in shallow water. When choosing a soil mix, pick one specifically formulated for Sundew or mix your own from 3 parts ground sphagnum moss to 1 part sand and/or perlite. Note: I list several sources for carnivorous plants and supplies in the Resources section at the back of this book.

Butterworts

Butterworts (*Pinguicula* species) are a little different than Sundew. They are not bog plants and don't like to grow in standing water. In the wild, Mexican varieties grow in moss, on the sides of cliffs, or on tree trunks. The soil mix should be very sandy and well draining. A good mix is 1 part each of peat moss, coarse sand, and perlite. What is different about Butterworts compared to other CPs is that they are only carnivorous in the summer. In the winter, their leaves lose their sticky dew and become more like a succulent. Because of this, their care changes a bit from summer to winter. In the summer months, keep them in a warm, humid environment with 12 to 14 hours of light per day. In a terrarium that means keeping the lid on and placing it in a brightly lit location. During the winter months they like to be kept slightly dryer and cooler. You can remove the lid during this time so that water evaporates more quickly. Also reduce light to about 8 to 10 hours per day. Butterworts flower during the winter months, making it worth the little bit of extra work. Both Butterworts and Sundew produce long flower stalks with single or multiple blooms, often in white, pink, or purple. They can last several weeks and are beautiful to look at.

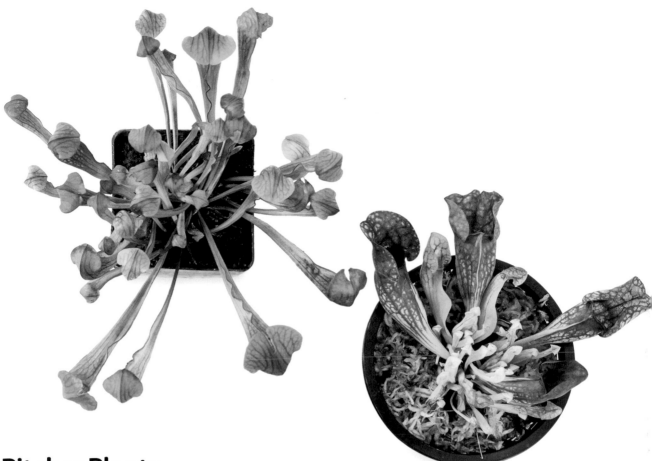

Pitcher Plants

Two other plants worth mentioning are *Sarracenia* 'Bugbat' and *Sarracenia purpurea*, both of which can do well in a large terrarium. The good thing about them, besides their stunning colors, is that both types stay relatively small, typically reaching a maximum height/width of about 12 inches (30.5 cm). The disadvantage is, unlike the tropical CPs I've mentioned so far, they *do* need a winter dormancy period and are therefore slightly more work. During this time, several of the pitchers may turn brown and die, making the plant temporarily look a little sickly. But if you are willing to give them the extra care they need and overlook their scraggly appearance a few months of the year, Pitcher Plants reward you by being interesting and unique terrarium inhabitants. *Sarracenia* plants need full sun for at least 6 hours in the summer and much cooler temperatures and lower amounts of light in the winter.

Since *Sarracenia* plants need to go dormant in the winter for the health of the plant, see "Project 9: Carnivorous Plant Terrarium" for detailed instructions on providing a proper dormancy period.

Marvelous Mini Tropical Plants

Tropical plants are those that come from hot and humid regions of the world. Generally they grow close to the forest floor and are shaded by trees throughout the day, receiving only filtered light from the sun. This makes them excellent houseplants. Some even enjoy living in a covered terrarium.

Tropical Plant Care

Most tropical plants like soil that's constantly damp, but not drenched with water (think about the rainforest where they're from). Use a potting soil mix with some added perlite to help aerate the soil and allow oxygen to reach the roots. This will also reduce the risk of root rot. Tropical plants like the high humidity inside a terrarium. Filtered or bright, but indirect, sunlight is best.

MY TOP 5 LIST OF TROPICAL PLANTS I'VE USED IN TERRARIUMS WITH SUCCESS IS AS FOLLOWS:

1. Emerald Ripple Peperomia (*Peperomia caperata*) has heart-shaped, wrinkled leaves. Readily roots from stem cuttings.

2. Jewel Orchids (*Macodes petola, Ludisia discolor, Ludochilus* sp.) terrestrial orchids with uniquely veined leaves. Plant the shallow roots in pure sphagnum moss or a well aerated peat-based soil (50 percent perlite, 50 percent peat). Do not use soil with fertilizer; instead use a diluted foliar fertilizer spray once a month.

3. Nerve Plant (*Fittonia albivenis*) has striking leaf pattern with white or pink veining. Adapts very well to terrarium life. Does not like to dry out.

4. Strawberry Begonia (*Saxifraga stolonifera*) grows in a circular pattern around a center point that will eventually send out long, thin runners that end in new baby clusters of leaves.

5. Friendship Plant (*Pilea mollis*) has green fuzzy leaves that fade to dark purple at the center. The leaves are also deeply wrinkled, which make it an interesting addition to any terrarium. You can make more of these plants by taking cuttings of the stems.

Beautiful Bonsai—Tiny Trees

Bonsai are miniature versions of the trees you see outside. Traditionally they are grown in small pots outdoors and are continuously trimmed and trained throughout their long lifetime. There are not too many types of bonsai trees that do well indoors, and even fewer that are good to use in terrariums, but there are a few!

Here are some of my favorite plants to turn into bonsai trees:

Ginseng Ficus

The first, and possibly easiest, is the Ginseng Ficus (*Ficus retusa*). Although it looks like a miniature tree, the trunk is actually the top half of the roots that grow aboveground. It has shiny, dark green, oval leaves. When planting, use an all-purpose houseplant soil and add a little extra perlite to the mix to improve water movement in the soil. Ginseng Ficus do not like to dry out very much between watering but be careful not to keep the soil soaking wet. Generally this means watering every few weeks, although in a terrarium you should be able to stretch the time between watering to a month or more. A bright spot next to a window is a good spot for this tree so that it can get the light it needs.

Brazilian Rain Tree

The Brazilian Rain Tree (*Pithecellobium tortum*) has leaves that look a lot like a Sensitive Plant (*Mimosa pudica*). And much like the Sensitive Plant, the leaves of the Brazilian Rain Tree droop and close when touched (though not with quite as much drama). It also does this at night when the Sun goes down. If it's happy, the tree produces fragrant white flowers that look like puffy balls in the spring or summer. Watch out, though, because the trunk has several long spines.

Brazilian Rain Tree Care

These great little trees like the soil to stay damp but not sopping wet, which could lead to root rot. On the other hand, if the soil dries out too much, it causes the leaves to turn yellow and fall off. Keep your Brazilian Rain Tree in the brightest location possible; it is a sun lover.

For more information on training, pruning, planting, and caring for a bonsai tree terrarium, visit "Project 3: Bonsai Terrarium" on page 58.

Outstanding Orchids

Orchids are popular plants because they have beautiful and unusual flowers that last a long time, up to several months in some cases. There are two main types of orchids: epiphyte and terrestrial. Epiphytes grow on other surfaces, such as tree branches, and terrestrial orchids grow in the ground. The ones you see in stores are usually epiphytes. Although they are grown in pots, they're growing in big chunks of bark because their roots are used to growing in the air and not in soil.

Orchid Care

With epiphytic orchids, fill your terrariums with bark chunks specifically made for orchids or use LECA balls made from clay (see chapter 2). I like using LECA in terrariums for my Lady Slipper Orchids because it helps keep their roots moist but allows lots of air and water drainage as well.

Terrestrial orchids, as mentioned, grow in the ground, but their roots don't go deep into the soil. Instead they tend to have roots that spread wide and grow in the fallen leaves on top of the soil. Jewel Orchid is one example of a terrestrial species. These types of orchids need an airier, well-draining soil mix, but they like to stay moister than the epiphytic kind. Terrestrial orchids shouldn't be left to dry out completely between watering. Use pure sphagnum moss as a substrate or a mix of 50 percent peat and 50 percent perlite.

In general, orchids like humidity, which make them a good candidate for terrariums; just be careful not to overwater them and try to give them some airflow by planting them in an open top jar or, if you're using a covered jar, keep the lid slightly opened. Orchids do well in low to medium light; any bright room will do. Keep the roots damp, but do not let them sit in water or they will rot. Fertilize using a foliar spray at half the recommended dose. Soil fertilizer additives are available for orchids, but I don't recommend them for terrarium use because there is no drainage and the fertilizers can build up too easily and end up killing the plant.

LADY SLIPPER ORCHIDS

One of my personal favorites to use in terrariums are the *Paphiopedilum* species, or Lady Slipper Orchids. They are stunning when in bloom! The *P. maudiae* types have interesting mottled foliage, so they look pretty even when they're not in bloom. The flowers on these species last between 1 to 2 months, possibly longer, and occasionally even bloom twice in the same year.

HOW TO TAKE CARE OF YOUR TERRARIUM

How do I water my terrarium?
Do I need to feed my plants?
How can I keep my plants looking their best?
What do I do if I see a bug in my terrarium?

All living plants go through a cycle of life. Baby leaves mature into adult leaves, and, after a time, old leaves start to turn brown and drop off a plant. New growth soon emerges from the stem and the cycle repeats itself as your plant grows. A few yellow or brown leaves here and there is normal and nothing to worry about. But there are several things you can do to keep your terrarium looking its best. In this chapter, I'll discuss what those things are and the tools to use to take care of your terrarium.

Terrarium Tools for Maintenance

The most useful and important items in your terrarium toolbox are a fine mist spray bottle, small watering can, long aquarium tongs, a small natural bristle brush, and scissors. Watering will be what you do most often. Let's learn a little about the water cycle and how to provide the right moisture for your terrarium plants.

Watering Your Terrarium

How often you water your terrarium depends on several factors:

▸ the type of container you're using and whether or not it has a lid

▸ the types of plants in your terrarium

▸ the amount of sunlight your terrarium receives

Most indoor plants do not like to be kept too wet or too dry. Finding the right balance can be a challenge.

First, consider the type of terrarium container you are using. Does it have a lid? If so, the lid will trap in a lot of moisture and not allow it to escape through evaporation. Lidded terrariums need to be watered much less often than ones with no lid. I'll share more information on why in the next section.

Next, think about the needs of the plants you've chosen for your terrarium. Are they desert plants like cacti? Then they'll require much less water than plants that prefer damp conditions, such as mosses or ferns.

Finally, plants that are exposed to more sunlight need more frequent watering than those kept in the shade. Have you ever gotten very thirsty after being out in the sun? Plants also drink more water and "sweat" it out under the Sun's intense rays (this is called transpiration).

The Water Cycle

The water cycle is the natural process where water circulates from the Earth up into the atmosphere and back again. A lidded terrarium goes through a water cycle much like the one that exists in nature. First, when you water your terrarium by soaking the soil or spraying the leaves, it's like rain that falls from the sky. In the natural water cycle, this is called "precipitation." Next, the plant drinks up that water through its roots, or in some cases it absorbs the water directly through its leaves. After using what it needs, the plant releases excess water as water vapor through little pores on the leaves called "stomata." The process of plants releasing water vapor into the air is called "transpiration." At the same time, the soil is releasing more moisture into the air through evaporation. In the natural water cycle, the water vapor from transpiration and evaporation collects into clouds (called "condensation") and falls as more precipitation. Inside your terrarium, when there is an excess of moisture, you'll see droplets of water form on the side of the glass (condensation). Eventually this moisture drips back down into the soil to the roots of the plant just like rain, and the cycle starts again!

Terrariums with no lid go through a similar process, but much more water vapor is lost from the opening of the container through evaporation.

The way water circulates from the Earth up into the atmosphere and back again is called the "water cycle." Terrariums have a water cycle much like the natural one.

HOW OFTEN TO WATER

How often you water your terrarium depends on the type of plants you're growing and the type of container the plants are in. In chapter 3, each plant type featured has information about how much water it prefers. Use that as a guide to create a watering schedule. Some covered terrariums can go months—or even years!—without being watered. Another tip is to touch the soil. If it's still damp, then you don't need to water quite yet.

WHAT KIND OF WATER?

The type of water you use in your terrarium is very important. The best kind to use is distilled. You can find gallon jugs of distilled water at a grocery store. Water from the tap contains chemicals, such as chlorine and hard minerals, that can quickly build up in a terrarium container. These can be harmful to your plants in a very short period of time. Tap water may also leave stains on glass surfaces, blocking your view of the plants and stopping sufficient light from entering the terrarium.

Feeding Your Terrarium Plants

In nature, most plants receive the food they need from the soil. They absorb these nutrients through their root system and use them to grow big and strong. But how do the nutrients get into the soil? It happens when dead leaves, animal waste, and other natural materials fall to the forest floor. Then tiny decomposing microbes and insects on and in the soil recycle this decaying matter, depositing it back into the earth. This is called the "nutrient cycle" because the plants can then absorb these nutrients and the cycle continues year after year.

In a healthy terrarium, plants can be fed in one of two ways:

1. The first is by adding some living organisms into the terrarium to copy the natural nutrient cycle. When added to terrariums, tiny insects called springtails (see page 51) eat up mold and decaying plant matter and turn it into food the plants can use.

2. The second way is to fertilize. However, plants in a terrarium need to be fertilized in a much different way than normal houseplants or plants that grow in our gardens. That's because a terrarium is a tiny, closed habitat that doesn't allow excess nutrients to wash away like they do when it rains outside. If you use too much fertilizer, you'll harm the plants instead of helping them. This is why I usually recommend fertilizing terrariums using a foliar (leaf) spray at half of the strength recommended on the bottle. Some of the spray will drip down into the soil and the rest can be absorbed by the leaves of the plant. Just spritz the leaves and soil of your terrarium with this liquid plant food once every few months.

Giving Your Terrarium a Haircut

All living plants go through a growth cycle: fresh new growth matures into adult leaves, old leaves turn brown and drop off the plant, new growth then emerges, and the process repeats. This means that your terrarium will require some maintenance from time to time.

Tools for Terrarium Maintenance

TOOLS YOU WILL NEED:

- *long aquarium tweezers (for terrariums with small openings)*
- *sharp scissors that have been disinfected*
- *spray bottle filled with distilled water*

Step-by-Step Terrarium Trimming

Step 1: Start by taking a look at your plants and making note of any stems or leaves that have turned yellow or brown. Snip them off with clean scissors and remove. Don't pull them off with your fingers; you may pull off more than you mean to.

Step 2: If you have moss in your terrarium, look for patches that are turning yellow or have brown tips. These can be trimmed with a scissors or pulled out with tongs. When moss starts to turn brown or yellow it can spread very quickly to the entire mat. Check your terrarium every week and remove any problem areas.

Step 3: Once you've removed all the dying stems and leaves, give your plants a quick misting with distilled water.

Step 4: Some plants will need to be divided from time to time. You may notice during maintenance that many plants (including succulents, Bromeliads, Tillandsias, and orchids) grow new baby plants at the base of the mother plant. Try to leave these babies attached until they are about half the size of their mother. When they're big enough, carefully separate and replant them by following the instructions in the next section.

CARING FOR SUCCULENTS AND LITHOPS

Caring for succulents and Lithops is a bit different. For these, especially in the case of Lithops, wait until the old leaves are 100 percent dry and crispy before removing them from the plant. That's because while a succulent leaf is decaying, the mother plant is reabsorbing all the stored water and nutrients from it. Of course, if a leaf falls off on its own, then feel free to remove it.

Making More Terrarium Plants

"Propagation" is the term used to describe the process of making new plants from ones you already have. The most well-known way to make more plants is by collecting and planting seeds. In this section, however, I'm not talking about starting with seeds. Instead I want to tell you how to make new plants by taking cuttings or by separating any baby plants that are growing from the mother plant.

Some plants, like this Peperomia caperata, *grow baby leaves under water.*

How to Separate Baby Plants

To propagate plants that produce their own babies, wait until the babies are big enough to survive on their own. That is usually when it reaches half the size of the adult. Then take sharp scissors that have been sterilized and snip the babies off at the base. In the case of air plants, you may be able to simply pull them off. Air plants don't need to be planted in soil, but for most plants, take the babies and place them on top of a container filled with some potting mix and nuzzle them in a little. Place them in a humid area and keep the soil moist, but not soaking wet. In a few weeks, with any luck, your baby plants will sprout roots of their own.

Air plants grow babies at their base after flowering.

How to Take Cuttings of a Terrarium Plant

To propagate a plant by stem cutting, use a pair of scissors to cut off a piece of plant stem with a leaf that's about 2 inches (5.1 cm) long. Place the bottom of the cutting in water that's no deeper than half the length of the stem. Some terrarium plants can be propagated by cutting off just a single leaf and stem, and some only grow new roots when there is a node present on the piece of stem. A "node" is the part of a plant where new leaves sprout from. It looks like a little bump or break in the stem. Trim the stem piece just below the node and place in water. You could also use LECA pebbles to anchor the cutting in the water container. Place the cutting in a bright location away from direct sunlight and extreme temperatures. Replenish the water over the next few weeks as it evaporates. Once your cutting has lots of long, heathy roots, remove it from the water and plant in soil. Place your new plant in a humid location (like a terrarium) so it has an easier time getting started.

TERRARIUM PLANTS TO PROPAGATE

- *Echeveria* (all types)
- *Tillandsia* (Air Plants)
- *Peperomia caperata* (Emerald Ripple Peperomia)
- *Pilea peperomioides* (Chinese Money Plant)
- *Greenovia dodrantalis* (Mountain Rose Succulent)
- *Macodes petola* (Jewel Orchid)
- *Pinguicula* (Butterworts)
- *Ficus pumila* (Creeping Fig)
- *Saxifraga stolonifera* (Strawberry Begonia)
- *Pilea mollis* (Friendship Plant)

Bugs in the Terrarium

Would you believe me if I told you that there are good bugs and bad bugs? Bugs that are considered bad are those that eat your plants or do damage to them in some way. Some of the bad guys include aphids, mealybugs, thrips, spider mites, scale, whiteflies, and fungus gnats. Slugs and snails, although not bugs, also do damage to plants. Other bugs, including spiders, ladybugs, lacewings, and many others, are good for your plants because they eat the harmful ones and keep them from getting out of hand.

What should you do if you find undesireable bugs in your terrarium? Some of them can be removed by hand (or with tongs) and released outside. Others are a little harder to get rid of. For fungus gnats and whiteflies, I use sticky traps made specifically for houseplants (have an adult find them at a plant store or online). They are usually yellow in color and have a very sticky surface that invites flying bugs to land and then get stuck. I leave the sticky trap in the infected terrarium for about 2 weeks just to make sure they've all been caught. You may need to repeat this process if eggs were laid and more insects hatch.

For other "bad bugs," you can either introduce a few good insects into the terrarium to eat them, squish them with your fingers, or ask an adult to use a solution of water, Neem oil, and a drop of dish soap to spray your plants. However, do not spray any products on carnivorous plants or moss. Try to keep any sprays off the glass (they can be tough to clean off the glass) and target them only on the plants.

Prevention is the best way to deal with unwanted pest insects. Inspect your plants before they go into the terrarium. Rinse the leaves under water to remove any pests or eggs that may be on them. Remove as much of the old soil as possible. That is where many bugs hide and lay eggs. Taking these steps beforehand may save you a lot of work later on.

Springtails in a holding container with horticultural charcoal and water.

THE BIOACTIVE TERRARIUM

Good bugs are beneficial to your plants—and I highly recommend putting some in your terrarium! They will do much of the clean-up work for you and, best of all, keep mold and fungus away. My favorite beneficial insects are called springtails. They are teeny-tiny white or tan insects that live in the top layer of soil. They come out in search of decaying leaves and mold or fungus gobble it up, and then poop out a fertilizer your plants can use to grow strong. They do not escape and are so small you will have to look very closely to see them. But they make a huge impact on the health of your terrarium. I have included some resources at the back of the book for ordering springtails online.

There are a few other beneficial bugs that are good for clean-up, but they're a little bigger and can be kept in your terrarium as pets.

- Isopods, sometimes called pill bugs, come in a variety of colors and make a great addition to your bioactive terrarium.
- Millipedes also do a good job of clean-up but can occasionally also munch on healthy leaves. (Do not confuse centipedes for millipedes; they may look similar, but centipedes are carnivorous and may even bite while millipedes are herbivorous and are very gentle and incapable of biting people.)

Now that we've taken a look at how to plant and care for a terrarium, I'm going to share some of my favorite terrarium projects with you in the next chapter. You'll learn step-by-step how to make these fun and creative terrariums with your family.

TERRARIUM PROJECTS
Winter Scene Terrarium

MATERIALS

- *Square acrylic canister or cookie jar with lid*
- *Live Rock Cap Moss (Dicranum) and 2 to 3 pieces of Cushion Moss (Leucobryum)*
- *HO-scale figures*
- *3 to 5 mini bottlebrush pine trees*
- *Coco coir or ground peat moss*
- *Small and medium pebbles/rocks*
- *Faux snow, white glitter, or fine white sand*
- *Long aquarium tongs*
- *Scoop*
- *Adjustable spray bottle filled with distilled water*
- *Paper towels*
- *Wide paintbrush*
- *Scissors*
- *Large mixing bowl (optional, for mixing coco coir)*
- *Springtails (optional, but highly recommended)*

Wintertime in many areas means long cold months covered in snow and not a green plant in sight. That is the perfect time to work on terrarium projects! And what better way to start off on your terrarium-making journey than to do a winter wonderland scene! For this project we use live moss, miniature figurines, and fake snow. At the back of this book in the Resources section, I include a list of sources for miniature figurines. I generally use ones that are HO scale (1:87 scale), which is how figures are measured for miniature railroad models. There are quite a few companies that make miniatures in this scale with various themes. The O scale or G scale models are slightly larger.

Step 1: If growing in coco coir, place the coco coir brick in a bowl and add distilled water. Let it soak for up to 1 hour until the brick is saturated (it will triple in size). It is then ready to use. If using ground peat moss, no preparation is necessary. Scoop the soil of choice into your container and pat it down at a slope, higher in the back and lower in the front. Try to get as straight a line as possible at the front by flattening it with your fingers or a flattening tool.

Step 2: Sweep away any soil that has stuck to the sides of the container with a small brush. You can also use your spray bottle set to a heavy stream to wash away stubborn debris from the sides of the jar.

Step 3: At the back of the jar, plant the Rock Cap Moss by gently nuzzling it into the soil. There is no need to cover the rhizoids (which are the moss version of roots) with soil. You just want the brown-colored bottom portion to be touching the soil and out of sight. If your moss has a lot of brown on the bottom, you can cut some of it off with scissors. Moss grows very differently than most plants and gets all the moisture and nutrients it needs from the air and via rainfall, absorbing everything through its tiny leaves. This is why watering moss is done through misting with a spray bottle instead of pouring water into the soil. Snipping off the bottom of the moss doesn't hurt it.

4

5

7

Step 4: Now take the pieces of Cushion Moss and place them on the soil at the front of the container, leaving a small gap between pieces. Press gently but firmly into place, nuzzling them into the soil as you did in the last step. Add some small pebbles and rocks between the two types of mosses in a few spots, which will add to the illusion of a miniature landscape.

Step 5: Next, place the mini bottlebrush trees into the scene at various levels. Push the bases down into the moss to hold them in place.

Step 6: Take glitter, fake snow, or the sand and pour a small amount in the gap between the Cushion Moss. Add a bit more here and there so it looks like it just lightly snowed. Wipe any stray bits away with your brush.

Step 7: Now put the figures into the scene. To help them stand upright, choose the flattest areas or nuzzle their feet into the moss. At this stage you can also add springtails by gently pouring them onto the moss, and they will go to work from there. (See the section on bugs in chapter 4 for more information.) Cover the container, place your terrarium in a bright location away from direct sunlight, and enjoy!

HOW OFTEN SHOULD YOU WATER MOSS?

In a closed jar, watering can be done by misting once every 6 to 8 weeks or so. You don't want to spray so much that it is pooling at the bottom but, enough so all plant surfaces get some water.

Hanging Glass Globe with Succulents

MATERIALS

- Hanging glass orbs
- 4-inch (10.2 cm) round plastic pot, empty (optional)
- Rosette succulents such as Sempervivum or Echeveria
- Succulent soil mix
- Sand
- Gravel
- Reindeer Moss
- Watering can
- Small scoop

Rosette succulents are some of the easiest plants to care for and are perfect for kids (and adults!) of all ages. The key to their care is to avoid overwatering and to give them a lot of light. The more light they get, the more brilliantly colored they will become. Succulents don't like to be in full sun quite as much as cacti do, so although they do appreciate bright light, they can burn if left in the scorching sun for a prolonged period of time. A great place for them is a sunny windowsill facing south, east, or west.

1

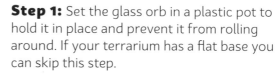

Step 1: Set the glass orb in a plastic pot to hold it in place and prevent it from rolling around. If your terrarium has a flat base you can skip this step.

Step 2: Scoop in a thin layer of gravel. This will be your drainage layer where any extra water will go. Remember, succulents don't need to be watered often and their roots don't like to sit in wet soil. Always wait until the soil is dry before watering again.

Step 3: Now add a layer of succulent soil mix a few inches (5 cm) deep. Make sure your mix has lots of sand and/or perlite for proper drainage and aeration.

2

3

4

Step 4: Remove the succulent from its pot and gently rinse its roots under running water while removing much of the existing soil from the root ball. You don't need to remove all the old soil, but if you do that's okay too. Untangle the roots slightly if they are still in the shape of the pot.

Step 5: Dig a small hole at the center of the soil and place the plant into the terrarium, then cover the roots with fresh soil. Pat down the soil around the base of the plant. Pour in a small amount of water.

Step 6: Add a thin layer of sand over the soil. Pick any color you like; you can even layer several colors if there is enough space to do so.

Step 7: Place a few pieces of Reindeer Moss in some of the gaps and add some small pebbles for decoration. Attach some jute rope to the glass and hang in a brightly lit location.

Bonsai Terrarium

MATERIALS

- ▶ Brazilian Raintree (Pithecellobium tortum)
- ▶ Large glass bell jar measuring approx. 12 inches (30.5 cm) high by 10 inches (25.4 cm) wide or larger
- ▶ 4 to 6 cups (950 ml to 1.8 L) of soil mix (half all-purpose potting mix and half sand or perlite)
- ▶ Scoop
- ▶ Gravel
- ▶ Decorative rocks; 1 large and several small
- ▶ 6 to 8 small pieces of Cushion Moss (Leucobryum glaucum)
- ▶ Sharp scissors
- ▶ Spray bottle
- ▶ Small watering can
- ▶ Soft bonsai wire

Bonsai are trees that are grown in a small pot that restricts the roots and keeps the tree in a miniature form. Bonsai trees' branches are also regularly trimmed to give them a unique shape. When making a bonsai terrarium, you will need to consider the needs of the tree before choosing one. See the bonsai tree section in chapter 3 for some good choices. The soil should not be left to dry out or the leaves will start to yellow and fall off, which means a covered jar is perfect because it will capture moisture inside and prolong the time needed between watering.

Step 1: Remove the bonsai plant from its pot by gently wiggling it while pulling in an upward motion. Be careful of the spines that grow from its trunk and branches. If there is a lot of resistance or you can't get it out of the pot, try squeezing the pot a little in a few places to dislodge any roots or soil stuck to the inside. Once you have your tree out of the pot, you may need to very gently break up the root ball if the roots still hold the shape of the pot even after being removed. Set the plant aside while you work on the next step.

Step 2: In the bottom of the tray, scoop in a thin layer of gravel up to about 1 inch (2.5 cm) high and flatten it with your hands. Make sure it's free of dust by rinsing it prior to use.

Step 3: Add just a small amount of soil around the center of the tray. This layer doesn't need to go all the way to the edge of the tray and should be about 1 inch (2.5 cm) high.

Step 4: Place the root ball of your tree slightly offcenter on top of the soil layer you just made.

Step 5: Add more soil all around the root ball, making a small hill and packing it down with your hands as you go. Continue to add soil all the way to the edge of the tray, lower around the edges and higher toward the center hill. Make sure you don't have it too high at the edges because you will be adding one more layer to that area. If the soil seems to be crumbling and won't stay in place, give it a thorough spray with your water bottle.

Step 6: Now place the largest rock to the side of the hill and gently nuzzle it into the soil. Take the smaller rocks and place them randomly in front of the hill.

Step 7: Scoop in gravel all around the rocks in front of the bonsai; leave the hill itself bare.

Step 8: Add the Cushion Moss piece by piece, covering the hill on all sides. Cut small pieces of wire and bend them in the shape of the letter U, then push them down into the moss as needed to keep the pieces from falling or moving around. Eventually the moss will adhere to the substrate and you can remove the wire if desired. Fill in any bare spots with gravel or small pieces of rock.

Step 9: Now you can test the design by placing the bell jar dome over the scene. If any branches are touching the glass, trim those back with a scissors. You will continue to trim as needed in the future to maintain your bonsai because it will naturally want to outgrow the terrarium. Part of the fun of a bonsai terrarium is maintaining it!

Step 10: Now pour a small amount of water at the base of the tree; up to 1 cup (235 ml). As always, I recommend using distilled water for the health of your plants. Add springtails (see chapter 4) to keep the ecosystem healthy, then place the dome over the terrarium and place it in a brightly lit location.

Maintenance: Repeat watering with 1 cup (235 ml) distilled water as needed, probably once every month. Fertilizing can be done at this time as well.

TRIMMING AND TRAINING BONSAI TREES

Before you begin, decide on the shape you'd like your bonsai tree to be. There are several options like formal upright, informal upright, cascading, slanting, and windswept to name a few. Trim off any long branches with pruning scissors. Use bonsai wire wrapped around to branches to slowly mold the tree into shape.

Pet Marimo Moss Ball Aquarium

MATERIALS

- Glass bowl
- Gravel (rinsed in a strainer to remove dust and debris that will cloud the water)
- Sea fan (small)
- Seashells
- Decorative rock
- 1 to 3 small Marimo moss balls
- Scoop for gravel

They're so fuzzy and cute, just like having a tiny aquatic pet! Marimo moss balls (*Aegagropila linnaei*) are very easy to care for and a lot of fun too. Even though they're called moss, in reality they are a rare type of freshwater algae that naturally grows in the shape of a ball. They live a long time and grow very slowly. But when a moss ball does grow up, it can reach up to 8 to 12 inches (20 to 30 cm) in diameter!

Step 1: Fill the bottom of the bowl with about 1 inch (2.5 cm) of the rinsed gravel.

Step 2: Next, place the sea fan upright at the back of the bowl. You may need to trim it with a scissors in order to make it fit.

Step 3: Place the decorative rock to one side in front of the sea fan. Then place the shells randomly on the gravel.

Step 4: Gently pour in the water until it is about ½ inch (1.3 cm) from the rim of the opening. You want to pour the water in slowly, so the gravel and decorations aren't disturbed too much. A small watering can may be helpful for this task. Any type of water can be used, even tap water. Personally I like to use distilled water for all my plants, including my Marimos. Tap water tends to leave a mineral ring along the glass when the water starts to evaporate, and that can be very hard to remove. Tap water also has a lot of chemicals that won't necessarily kill moss balls but may keep them from thriving. I do use tap water when rinsing my Marimos and washing out the container.

Step 5: Rinse your Marimos under running water, then place them into the bowl. Play with your moss balls by poking them or moving them around with a chopstick, but it's best not to remove them from the water. If they are left to completely dry out, they will not survive.

HOW TO CARE FOR MARIMO MOSS BALLS

To provide the proper environment for your moss ball, find a location that receives medium indirect light. Choose a spot that's in a brightly lit room or close to a lamp with a florescent or LED bulb. However, do not keep your Marimo ball in direct sunlight. If you notice brown patches, that usually means it is getting too much light. But it can also mean the water is too warm, so try to find a cool location to place the aquarium bowl.

You will need to top off the water once every 2 to 3 weeks due to evaporation. Cleaning can be done once a month. At that time, rinse the gravel and wipe down the glass where other types of algae may start to grow. I also run the Marimos under a soft stream of cold water and gently squeeze them to remove any dirt particles that have been trapped inside. When you first put them back into the bowl, they may float for a day or two but don't worry; it's just air that is trapped inside and they will sink again soon.

Geometric Terrarium with Succulents, Crystals, and Geodes

MATERIALS

- Geometric glass container with an open top
- Succulent/cactus potting mix
- Gravel or horticultural charcoal for drainage layer
- Black sand (or any color of your choice)
- Amethyst, or another type of crystal or geode
- Agate slice
- 3 small to medium-sized succulents or cacti (in 2- to 4-inch [5.1 to 10.2cm] pots)
- Watering can
- Tongs
- Small scoop
- Small paintbrush

A fun way to display crystals, geodes, or even fossils is to pair them with plants in a terrarium. For this project we will be planting an open-faced geometric bowl with drought-hardy succulents. Succulents are easy to care. They don't need to be watered very often compared to other types of plants. They also have interesting shapes and colors, and some even blush bright red in the sun.

BEST PLANT PICKS

This terrarium contains:

- Turkish Stonecrop (*Rosularia platyphylla*)
- String of Pearls (*Senecio rowleyanus*)
- Zebra Haworthia or Pearl Plant (*Haworthia pumila* or *Tulista pumila*)

Step 1: Add about 1 inch (2.5 cm) of gravel or horticultural charcoal to the bottom of the container for drainage. Because the terrarium has no drainage hole in the bottom, be careful not to overwater your plants. Providing a drainage layer helps keep any excess water out of the soil and away from the roots. Succulents and cacti commonly develop root rot if too much water sits in the soil for too long, so it's important not to skip this step.

Step 2: Fill the container with a pre-mixed succulent/cactus potting soil. Leave ½ inch (1.3 cm) between the soil and the rim of the container. Flatten it by patting down with your hands.

Step 3: Dig a hole at the back-left side of the container that is about the same size as your tallest and largest plant's pot (I have used a Zebra Haworthia). Remove the plant from its pot and gently untangle some of the roots while removing some of the existing potting soil from the root ball. You don't have to remove all the soil but remove enough so that some of the roots are hanging free. Do this very gently if the plant has very thin, delicate roots. Try not to break any roots off the plant, though if a small piece or two accidentally falls off it should still be okay. Now place the ball into the hole, cover any exposed roots with soil, and gently pat down.

Step 4: At the front left side, dig a small hole for the String of Pearls and repeat the same process as in step 3. Allow some of the "pearls" to hang over the edge of the bowl. As this plant grows longer, you can take cuttings and propagate them to make new plants. Succulents are best propagated by placing the cuttings on top of moist soil and keeping it in a humid area until you see roots start to grow. In the case of String of Pearls, make sure some of the stem is touching the soil so that the new roots know where to go. See chapter 4 for more details on propagation.

Step 5: To plant the Turkish Stonecrop, dig another hole just opposite the String of Pearls at the front right of the container and repeat step 3. (Note that the roots of this plant are usually very thin so be careful not to break them off.)

Step 6: Even out the soil layer by flattening it with your hands. Then using a small scoop, cover the remaining surface with a thin layer of sand. Use a bristly paintbrush to sweep out any sand that gets stuck in the centers of the plants' leaves.

Step 7: Place the largest crystal or geode at the back right of the container. Then randomly place the other crystals and the agate slice into the terrarium.

Bromeliad Terrarium with Layered Sand

MATERIALS

▶ *Wall planter with glass front (see the Resources section)*

▶ *Fine sand and/or gravel in 2 to 3 colors (for this example, I used black, red, and white)*

▶ *Ground peat moss or all-purpose potting soil*

▶ *3 to 5 live Earth Star (Cryptanthus) Bromeliads measuring 2 to 4 inches (5.1 to 10.2 cm)*

▶ *Spray bottle*

▶ *Small scoop*

▶ *Watering can*

Terrariums and plants are fun to care for and are also nice items to decorate with. For this project we will be using round wall planters with a glass panel that allows the soil mix to be shown. By using colored sand, aquarium gravel, or a combination of both, you can create a unique and attractive home for plants.

A plant I like to use for these types of terrariums is a bromeliad called *Cryptanthus* or Earth Star. They are like air plants in that they absorb a lot of the moisture and nutrients they need through their leaves. However, unlike air plants, they grow in the ground and their roots are a little more sophisticated than their epiphyte cousins. They like a lot of moisture in the air, with a relative humidity of 40 to 60 percent or higher. Therefore, when choosing a spot to hang this wall terrarium pick one that is away from fans or air vents.

1

2

Step 1: Using a scoop, fill the bottom of the wall planter with (in this example) black sand to a depth of about 2 to 3 inches (5 to 7.5 cm). Follow with a thin layer of the white, then the red sand. Pour it in thicker in some areas and thinner in others to create "hills" of color.

Step 2: Now scoop in a 1- to 2-inch (2.5 to 5.1 cm) layer of peat-based soil on top of the sand. Dig shallow holes where the plants will go, making sure they are several inches (5.1 cm) apart.

Step 3: Set aside the wall planter. Prepare your plants by removing them from their pots (if any) and gently untangle the roots, removing as much potting soil as possible. Next, rinse the roots under running water to remove the rest of the soil.

3

Step 4: Place each plant, one at a time, into the holes and turn them so they are slightly facing toward you. Then take a small amount of soil and cover the roots, patting down gently to keep them in place. Water lightly while holding the wall planter over the sink. Try not to pour water in too fast because you don't want mud to come pouring out everywhere. Using too much water can also disturb the sand layers below, so go slowly. If you water correctly then no excess should drip out of the container.

Step 5: Hang the finished terrarium in a bright spot with lots of humidity, such as a kitchen or bathroom with a window. Do not place in direct sunlight because the leaves will burn, but the brighter the indirect light is, the more vibrant an Earth Star's colors will be.

CRYPTANTHUS CULTIVARS FOR YOUR TERRARIUM

- Ruby Port
- Pink Star
- Absolute Zero

- Bivittas Ruby
- Frostbite

Japanese Garden with Living Rocks

MATERIALS

▶ *Glass half-bowl*

▶ *Succulent soil*

▶ *Scoop*

▶ *Small paintbrush*

▶ *Chopstick*

▶ *Gravel or horticultural charcoal*

▶ *10 to 15 Lithops of various sizes (see the Resources section)*

▶ *Sand (for fun, pick colored sand)*

▶ *Sand stamps*

▶ *Japanese lantern/pagoda figurine*

Lithops are called "Living Rocks" for a good reason. Where they grow in the wild, they look very much like stones on the ground. In fact, their camouflage is so good many people don't even see them as they walk by. But if you look closely, you will discover this little succulent plant comes in a wide variety of pretty colors and patterns. They also flower once a year, and the blooms are dazzling!

Step 1: Pour a thick, 2- to 3-inch (5.1 to 7.5 cm) drainage layer of horticultural charcoal or gravel into the bowl. Flatten with your hand. This layer will help if you accidentally overwater your Lithops.

Step 2: Scoop in succulent soil mix until it reaches a height of about ½ inch (1.3 cm) below the rim of the bowl, and pack it down so it's flat.

Step 3: Use the chopstick to dig a small hole in the soil about 1 inch (2.5 cm) deep for larger Lithops and ½ inch (1.3 cm) deep for smaller ones. I find doing one at a time is easiest.

Step 4: Insert the roots of the plant into the hole and pack down the soil around its base. Make sure about one-half to three-quarters of the base of the Lithops is also inserted into the soil. They tend to push up a little as they grow, so placing them a bit deeper into the soil than you ultimately want them to be is helpful. Try to get the roots as straight as possible because whatever angle they go in will also be the direction they grow.

5

6

Step 5: Continue until you have planted them all in the design you want. Be creative; you can follow the design shown or do a different shape. A star, heart, or even animal shape is a fun way to personalize this project.

Step 6: Using the scoop, pour a layer of sand over the surface of the soil. Use the paintbrush to get in between and around the Lithops.

Step 7: Smooth the sand to get it as flat as possible.

Step 8: Use the sand stamps to make designs in the sand or use your chopstick to draw your own designs. Put the Japanese lantern figurine in the terrarium and place in a bright location. Enjoy!

7

8

GROWING NEW LEAVES

During the winter, Lithops go through a big transformation. They completely shed their old leaves and a new plant grows from in between the old growth. You will start to notice the crack at the top widening and then the new leaves will start to show. During this time, don't water at all. Allow the old leaves to remain until they are completely brown and crispy because the new plant that's emerging is actually sucking up all the liquid from the old, shrinking leaves. When the old leaves are finally dried up, usually by spring, you can resume watering. Giving Lithops a bit more water in the springtime is okay; it will help with flower production. Three to 4 spoonsful per plant is appropriate.

MAINTAINING YOUR LIVING STONES

There are a few tricks to keep Lithops happy and healthy. First is light; they need to grow in a bright location. A good place to keep them is a sunny windowsill or under full-spectrum lights. If you can give them 4 to 5 hours per day in a sunny spot, they will be very happy.

Another trick to keep Lithops happy is to use a soil that drains well. They do not like their roots to stay wet and can quickly turn to mush if kept in damp soil for too long. A mix with 50 percent soil and 50 percent perlite, sand, or other gritty material is best. The last, and trickiest, part is watering. Lithops can store water for months in their leaves, and they are used to very dry conditions. Watering should be done only when the soil is bone dry and then only a spoonful or two of water per plant is necessary.

PROJECT 08

Geometric Terrarium with Air Plants

MATERIALS

- 3 to 5 small to medium-sized air plants
- Open geometric terrarium (no lid)
- Fine sand in any color
- Small driftwood branch
- Spray bottle filled with distilled water
- Small scoop
- Reindeer Moss
- Pebbles and rocks or shells to decorate

Air plants, or Tillandsias, are epiphytes, meaning they grow on the limbs and branches of trees as well as the sides of rocks or cliffs. They attach themselves to these surfaces by roots that are used for the sole purpose of hanging on. All the nutrients and moisture they require is absorbed through their leaves, so it makes sense that they generally grow in tropical, humid environments. An open terrarium is a good home for them because it helps keep some humidity around the plant but also allows airflow, which is important for Tillandsias.

Step 1: Scoop sand into the terrarium and fill to about 2 inches (5.1 cm) high.

Step 2: Put the small piece of driftwood at the back center of the terrarium. Try positioning it different ways until you find one you like.

Step 3: Next, place the tallest air plants at the back of the container and to one side, standing upright.

TILLANDSIA SPECIES FOR YOUR TERRARIUM

- *T. brachycaulos multiflora*
- *T. caput medusae*
- *T. butzii*
- *T. ionantha*
- *T. capitata*

Step 4: Arrange the medium-sized air plants in the middle either on top of, or right in front of, the driftwood. Place them on their sides so they are facing toward you. Then put the smallest one in the front, also facing you.

Step 5: Add some Reindeer Moss randomly to fill any large empty spaces, but leave the center front open so you can still see the sand.

Step 6: Spread a few rocks, shells, or pebbles in the sand for decoration. Place your terrarium in a location that receives bright but indirect light.

AIR PLANT TERRARIUM MAINTENANCE

This terrarium will not need a lot of maintenance compared to some of the others in this book. Air plants are easy to care for and have just a few requirements as discussed in their profile in chapter 3. I recommend watering weekly using the following method: remove the air plants from the terrarium and place them on newspaper or paper towels (anyplace that can get wet). Using a fine mist spray bottle filled with distilled water, thoroughly mist your plants, trying to avoid spraying down the center of the plant where water can pool. After all the leaves have been misted, let the plants sit out for 30 to 60 minutes. Then place them back into the terrarium.

Dinosaur Bones Diorama Terrarium

MATERIALS

▸ Large glass orb terrarium (at least 10 inches [25 cm] deep)

▸ 1 Little Tree Plant (Biophytum sensitivum)

▸ 1 Creeping Fig in 4-inch (10.2 cm) pot (Ficus pumila)

▸ 1 mini tropical plant of choice in 2-inch (5.1 cm) pot (optional)

▸ All-purpose peat-based potting soil

▸ Horticultural charcoal

▸ 1 cup (237 ml) black sand

▸ ½ cup (118 ml) white sand

▸ Small pebbles

▸ Tongs

▸ Spray bottle filled with distilled water

▸ Small scoop

▸ Dinosaur figurines

In this project we will create a miniature dinosaur fossil diorama much like the giant ones you see in museums. Whenever I go to the science museum near my home, I like to look at the giant displays of dinosaur skeletons and think about what it must have been like on Earth at that time. I imagine lots of tropical plants, flying insects the size of birds, and, of course, the dinosaurs. That is the inspiration for the design behind this project.

Step 1: Fill the bottom of the terrarium with a layer of horticultural charcoal, about 1 inch (2.5 cm) high. This will be a drainage layer where excess water can go. Charcoal also helps keep the terrarium substrate fresh.

Step 2: Scoop in several cups of potting soil so that it reaches a height of about 3 inches (7.6 cm). Keep the right side of the pile slightly lower than the left. Start building a mini hill on the left side with your hands.

Step 3: Continue to pile up soil on one side to form a hill and pat it down. Then dig a small hole at the center of the hill. This step will be easier if your soil is slightly damp.

Step 4: Remove the Little Tree Plant from its pot and place the root ball into the hole. Make sure its leaves are not sticking up so high that they touch the glass at the top. Nuzzle it down into the soil as needed to reach the right height. Now scoop in more soil around the base of the tree and keep building up the hill by patting it down with your hands. If the soil is crumbling and dry, spray it with water so it becomes a claylike consistency, which will help you form the hill. Make sure all of the tree's roots are covered. You now should have a hill with a tree and to the right, a lower flat area.

Step 5: Remove the creeping plant from its pot and gently untangle some of the roots while removing about half of the potting soil from the root ball. Try your best not to break off too many roots. Then dig a shallow hole to the right of the hill and place the plant into it. Use some extra soil to cover the roots. At this point many of the leaves may be covered in stray bits of soil; planting can be messy. To clean off the leaves and sides of glass, set your spray bottle to a hard stream and spray off the dirt, holding the nozzle a pencil's length away from the leaves (you don't want to blast them right off the stem!).

Step 6: Make sure all the soil is patted down and your hill is still in place. Spray the glass again, if needed, and then wipe the interior down with a paper towel.

Optional: A mini tropical plant placed randomly adds to the landscape you are creating. Pick something that might look like a small bush or random "weeds." Here I used a few stems of *Pilea glauca* Silver Sparkle. It easily roots from cuttings but will need to be trimmed frequently so it doesn't take over the terrarium.

Step 7: Using the small scoop, cover the hill area with a thin layer of black sand. Then make a path going from the front toward the back of the terrarium using white sand. Line the path randomly with small pebbles.

Step 8: Now place the dinosaur figures into the scene. Your miniature dino diorama is complete!

SPECIAL CARE FOR YOUR DINOSAUR TERRARIUM

Trim the Creeping Fig as needed; it tends to grow very quickly and can take over like many vining plants. The cuttings can be rooted if you want to make more plants. The Little Tree Plant, or *Biophytum*, closes its leaves when disturbed and will initially look droopy from planting. It also closes its leaves when the Sun goes down. During the day the leaves open again and it looks just like a tiny palm tree. Trim off any yellow fronds that appear at the bottom. Biophytums get tiny pinkish flowers on a spike, which are followed by a star-shaped seedpod. When a seedpod opens, it launches tiny brown seeds in every direction. They germinate very easily, so easily that this plant is considered a weed in its native habitat. If you prefer not to see tiny Biophytums popping up everywhere, snip off the seedpods with scissors before they open.

Carnivorous Plant Terrarium

MATERIALS

- House-shaped glass terrarium
- Horticultural charcoal
- 2 to 3 Sundew plants (Drosera burmannii, D. capensis, D. spatulata, or D. alicicae)
- 2 to 3 Mexican Butterwort plants (Pinguicula esseriana)
- 1 Sarracenia 'Bug Bat' Pitcher Plant (alternative: Sarracenia purpurea plant)
- Live sphagnum moss
- Long fiber sphagnum moss (dry)
- Scoop
- Scissors
- Brush
- Tongs
- Spray bottle filled with distilled water

Keeping a carnivorous plant falls somewhere between having a plant and having a pet. They are lots of fun to watch as they catch tiny insects as prey! Carnivorous plants, or CPs, come in a variety of bright colors and shapes (see chapter 3). Not only are the leaves of the plants colorful, but they have beautiful flowers too. Some even produce a sticky dew on their leaves that sparkle when the light hits them. We will be using some of these dewy, sparkly plants called Sundew for this project, along with Butterworts and Pitcher Plants.

Step 1: Check to see if your terrarium has a good seal at the base by pouring some water inside. If it leaks, either place it on a tray to catch excess water or use aquarium sealant to close the leak. Once the terrarium is ready to be planted, start with the *Sarracenia* 'Bug Bat' Pitcher Plant. Rinse the roots to remove the soil and cover them with damp long fiber sphagnum moss. Or, if your plant is already growing in a plastic basket pot with lots of holes, leave it in the container. This will allow the roots to easily soak up water as well as allow you to easily remove it later when it's in dormancy. Place the plant in the terrarium at the back right.

Step 2: Using a scoop, fill the bottom of the terrarium with horticultural charcoal to a depth of about 2 to 3 inches (5.1 to 7.6 cm). Avoid getting charcoal in the Pitchers themselves. Have the charcoal at a slant, slightly higher in the back than in the front. Though gravel could also be used, I prefer using charcoal because it keeps the terrarium smelling fresh and the water from going stagnant.

Step 3: Next dig a small hole in the charcoal to the left of the pitcher plant. Keeping the Sundew in its pot (2-inch [5 cm] plastic pots work best; make sure there are drainage holes in the bottom), place the plant in the hole.

Step 4: Add more horticultural charcoal to cover up the pot, being careful to avoid pouring it directly on the plants. If any charcoal lands on the sticky Sundew leaves, brush it off or use tongs to remove the stray pieces.

Step 5: Fill in any gaps with live sphagnum moss by placing it on top of the soil between plants. Plant it a little taller at the back than in the front of the container. Sphagnum does not have a root system, so simply placing it on top of the charcoal is fine.

Step 6: Take the Butterworts and, with tongs, gently place them on the live sphagnum near the front of the terrarium. The roots will eventually grow down into the moss so there is no need to push them down.

Step 7: Using a strong stream, spray the sides of the glass, pointing the stream downward so any bits of soil get cleaned off and pushed to the bottom. With tongs or a damp cotton swab, gently pick off debris that may have stuck to the plants. Pour in some distilled water until you have 1 or 2 inches (2.5 to 5.1 cm) at the bottom of the terrarium. Keep the water at that level all the time. Remember most of these carnivorous plants are bog plants that live in and around water; they do not like to dry out.

TAKING CARE OF A CP TERRARIUM

CPs like bright, direct light, so place your terrarium near a sunny window or under a lamp with full-spectrum light.

Never use tap water on CPs. They are very sensitive to the minerals and other chemicals present in tap water and will start to die soon after it is used. Instead use distilled or reverse osmosis water, which can be purchased at a grocery store.

HOW TO FEED CPs

There are two options when feeding these plants. You can give them a few tiny bugs, like flightless fruit flies, that can be purchased at pet stores or from places listed in the Resources section at the back of this book. Only one or two bugs per plant is necessary, and feed only about once, or at the most, twice, per month. Alternatively you can feed them using dry betta fish food flakes. When you feed fish food, do so just as sparingly as you would with live prey; feed only a few crushed flakes per plant once a month.

HOW TO PROVIDE A WINTER REST FOR YOUR CARNIVOROUS PLANT

Not all CPs need a winter rest period but *Sarracenia* (Pitcher Plants) do. In their natural habitat, they live where winters dip down below freezing. Because of this, they need a rest from actively growing for a few months out of the year (called a "dormancy"). Since we planted this terrarium with the plants still in their pots, it's easy to remove the *Sarracenia* for a short period and put it in a cooler location for this rest period. After removing the plant, rinse its roots under water and replace the existing long fiber sphagnum moss with a fresh bunch. Dampen the moss and wrap it loosely around the roots. Then place the plant in a plastic bag and put it in the fridge for about 2 months. Once that period of time has passed, remove the plant and place it back into the basket and into the terrarium. Some pitchers may turn brown and die off, but the plant is simply making room for fresh new growth. Snip off the dead pitchers near the base of the plant.

Vivarium for a Praying Mantis

MATERIALS

▶ *Large canning jar with screen lid (screen lids can be purchased separately, see Resources section)*

▶ *Fine gravel or sand, any color*

▶ *Reindeer Moss*

▶ *Small tropical plant in a 2-inch (5.1 cm) pot*

▶ *Stick or small branch*

▶ *Scoop*

▶ *Mini spray bottle*

▶ *Praying mantis*

▶ *Feeder insects*

A vivarium is a terrarium that is a home not just for plants but, for animals too. This project is home for a fascinating insect called a praying mantis. Praying mantises make fun and interesting pets and are easy to care for. There are a variety of different mantis species to choose from: brown ones, green ones, pink ones, and more. Some look like dead leaves while others look like flowers. I have kept many types of praying mantises as pets, and my personal favorite is the ghost mantis (*Phyllocrania paradoxa*). If the container is large enough and there is enough cover, they are one of the few species of mantises that can be kept in a small group. Most of the other types should be kept alone because they are carnivores, and they'll make a tasty meal of one another. For this project, we will be using a large jar with a screen lid, which is big enough to keep a single mantis.

Step 1: Leave your mini plant in the pot and place it in the jar toward the back. Try to use a tall, sturdy plant that reaches close to the top, so the mantis has something to climb on. Typically mantises stay toward the top of the jar, often hanging upside down. Since it will be difficult for it to grab onto the slippery glass, having the plant reach close to the top will help the mantis move around easily.

Step 2: Using a small scoop, pour the sand or gravel around the pot but not on top of the soil or plant. Fill to about 1½ inches (3.8 cm) or a bit below the top of the plant's pot.

Step 3: Insert the stick toward the front or side of the jar as an additional climbing post. A stick with a few small side branches is better than a straight one, as you are creating a mini jungle gym for your mantis.

TYPES OF PRAYING MANTISES TO KEEP AS PETS

- Ghost Mantis (*Phyllocrania paradoxa*)
- Spiny Flower Mantis (*Pseudocreobotra wahlbergii*)
- Orchid Mantis (*Hymenopus coronatus*)
- African Green Mantis (*Sphodromantis lineola*)
- See the Resources section for the names of insect farms that sell these species.

4

5

Step 4: Cover the sand or gravel layer with Reindeer Moss, enough to hide the pot. After you put the moss in the jar, push it down a little so it isn't taking up too much room. The terrarium should be less than half full; the mantis needs room to explore.

Step 5: It's now time to add your new pet! Gently pick up the mantis and let it crawl onto the stick (a very soft nudge might be necessary—just don't forget how small and fragile your new pet is!). Place the lid on the jar and put it in a warm spot away from direct sun or cold drafts. Every few days offer food and water (see the sidebar). When the mantis is very small, it could drown in water droplets so be sure to use a fine mist spray bottle and spray away from the mantis, just once or twice, onto the side of the glass or plant. If the mantis is thirsty it will drink. If not, don't worry because it also gets hydrated from the juicy bugs it eats (eew!).

HOW TO CARE FOR YOUR PRAYING MANTIS

Each type of mantis has different housing and care needs. The terrarium here is suitable both for ghost mantises and spiny flower mantises. Other mantises grow to be much larger and need a bigger container. Each type also has specific needs for humidity and temperature. A few good websites to read up on your mantis's specific needs are www.panterrapets.com and www.usmantis.com. These are also both excellent sources to buy your mantis and feeder insects!

When you first get your new pet, it will likely be a very small baby, or nymph. You will need to start by feeding it something small like flightless fruit flies. As it grows, start offering small crickets or flies, which are their favorite foods! To keep flies from escaping into the house, set the fly container in the fridge for a minute, then drop a fly into the terrarium. As soon as the fly warms up, it will start moving and attract the mantis's attention. See the Resources section at the back of the book for a list of places to buy feeder insects.

MAINTENANCE AND CLEANING

Water the plant inside your vivarium about once every week or two. After temporarily removing your mantis buddy, stick your finger down to touch the soil of the plant. If it feels dry, add a small amount of water. Try not to let a lot of water drain out of the pot into the bottom of the jar. I recommend adding no more than ¼ cup (60 ml) of water at a time and pouring it directly into the soil to avoid getting everything else wet.

About once a month, it's a good idea to completely clean the habitat. There may be mantis poop at the bottom or perhaps dead plant leaves. This is the reason why the plant is left in its pot instead of being planted directly in the jar. It makes cleanup easier. Remove any waste and wipe the glass with a damp paper towel (no soap or cleaning products, please!). Then put everything back in and return your mantis to his sparkling-clean home.

Closed Jungle Ecosystem with Tropical Plants

MATERIALS

▸ Glass cookie jar with lid

▸ Potting soil (premixed, made for indoor plants)

▸ Horticultural charcoal

▸ Small pebbles

▸ 2 large rocks

▸ 3 to 5 mini tropical plants in 2-inch (5.1 cm) pots

▸ Scoop

▸ Tongs

▸ Spray bottle filled with distilled water

▸ Springtails

▸ Mini animal figurine (optional)

Using miniature tropical plants in a terrarium gives you the widest range of shapes and leaf patterns to choose from. Best of all, tropical plants seem to be made for terrarium life. They come from rainforests and jungles where they grow on the forest floor, which is a shady and humid environment. It's easy to replicate those conditions within a covered glass jar placed in a bright room but away from direct sunlight. This project gives you some freedom in your choice of plants because you can either use the same ones listed or pick ones you like. Most plant nurseries carry what they call "fairy garden plants" or "miniature tropical plants" in 2-inch (5.1 cm) pots and will have a variety to choose from.

Step 1: Scoop horticultural charcoal into the bottom of the jar to a depth of about 1 inch (2.5 cm). This serves as a drainage layer and keeps the terrarium smelling fresh.

Step 2: Now add 3 inches (7.6 cm) of potting soil and slope it so that it is higher at the back of the jar than at the front. Pat it down lightly.

Step 3: Dig a small hole at the back of the jar and place the root ball of the tallest growing plant into it. Cover any exposed roots with soil and gently pack it down. Repeat this step for all the tall plants you have chosen to use.

BEST PLANT PICKS

When making a tropical plant terrarium, choose plants that prefer high humidity and low to medium light (nothing that needs full sun). The list of suitable plants is long: mini ferns, Peperomias, trailing Ficus, and so forth. For this project, I used five types: Strawberry Begonia (*Saxifraga stolonifera*), Nerve Plant (*Fittonia albivenis*), Peperomia Emerald Ripple (*Peperomia caperata*), String of Hearts (*Ceropegia woodii*), and a mini woodland fern. The more plants used, the faster the terrarium could become overcrowded so using fewer than these five listed is okay.

Step 4: Next, at the front of the terrarium where the lowest part of the slope is, dig a small hole, place a low-growing plant in it, and cover roots with soil, packing it down around the base. Any type of vining plant, such as String of Hearts, generally stays low and is a good choice for the foreground. Repeat this step with your other low-growing varieties. Leave a space between the background plants and foreground plants.

Step 5: Place large rocks randomly, in the middle ground and/or at the back of the terrarium, wherever you have left a space open.

Step 6: Fill in any leftover empty spaces where the soil is showing with small pebbles or sand. This is simply for decoration; there's no need to cover every bare spot.

Step 7: Set the spray bottle to a heavy stream and spray the sides of the glass inside the jar, pointing downward. Continue around the interior until all stray dirt has been washed to the bottom. Using a lighter mist, spray any leaves or rocks that need cleaning. Then take a paper towel and dry off the inside of the glass. Add springtails by pouring them in from the top. They will get right to work on keeping your terrarium healthy and clean. Optional: Place an animal figurine of your choice inside to create a mini jungle scene.

TAKING CARE OF YOUR TROPICAL TERRARIUM

This terrarium will need frequent haircuts because most tropical plants grow very quickly, especially when they are happy with their living conditions. Many of them can be propagated by trimming and putting the cuttings either in water or potting soil (see chapter 4). This means you can soon make more terrariums from the very same plants. Share your creations with your friends and family; terrariums make great gifts!

Orchidarium

 ## MATERIALS

- LECA pebbles, small bag, rinsed
- Open-top glass vase (no lid)
- Paphiopedilum maudiae Lady Slipper Orchid (see the Resources section)
- 2 to 3 Tillandsia air plants
- Driftwood or decorative branch
- Small scoop or measuring spoon
- Watering can
- Decorative stone
- Tongs

Orchids are some of the most beautiful and unusual flowering plants on Earth. They come in many different varieties and some of them are even suitable for terrarium life. There are two major groups of orchids: terrestrial, meaning they live on the ground, and epiphytes, which grow clinging to tree branches or rocks. Terrestrial Orchids are not as well known as their epiphyte cousins and grow in humus not soil. Humus is made up of fallen leaves and other decaying matter that lays on the surface of the ground in wooded areas. Jewel Orchids and Lady Slipper Orchids are two examples of terrestrial species. These do very well when planted in terrariums. Epiphytic Orchids are usually the kind you see at supermarkets growing in bark chips. Since this type grows clinging to trees high up in the forest canopy, their root system is very different than most plants. These types of orchids require a light, fast-draining potting medium (like bark chips) because they will rot if kept in normal soil. They also need a lot of airflow and can quickly die if kept in a closed terrarium.

Step 1: Using either your hand or tongs, grasp the plastic pot the Lady Slipper Orchid is growing in and lower it into the center of the base of the jar. Reposition leaves as needed so that they are not folded downward.

Step 2: Slowly scoop the rinsed LECA pebbles into the jar around the base of the pot until they reach the same level as the top of the plastic pot. Be very careful not to pour it directly on any flowers because they are fragile and can break off easily.

Step 3: Place the driftwood or decorative branch behind the orchid and nuzzle it down into the LECA slightly. You can reposition leaves as needed so they are not buried or damaged. Then place the decorative rock toward the front of the jar to one side.

Step 4: Using tongs, insert the air plants and place them at varying heights, one at "soil" level in front of the orchid and a few on the branch or driftwood.

Step 5: Now pour in about a half cup (118 ml) of distilled water around the base of the leaves. Never use tap water on your orchid. Do this again in about 2 to 3 weeks, depending on how quickly the medium dries out. If you see any fog or water droplets on the side of the glass where the LECA is, then you don't need to water. The LECA will also be a slightly darker color when it's moist than when it's dry. You do *not* want to see an accumulating pool of water at the base of the jar because standing water can cause the roots to rot.

See the sections on air plants and orchids in chapter 3 for long-term care tips.

ORCHID FLOWERS

Orchids are best known for their flowers, which are usually long-lasting and very colorful. *Paphiopedilum*, or the Lady Slipper types, have blooms that generally last about 2 months. You can snip off the flower stalk close to the base once it has withered. The process of growing a new flower will begin again in about a year. In the meantime, new baby leaves will grow from the base of the plant forming a clump of plants. New flowers will emerge from these offshoots.

REPOTTING YOUR ORCHID IN LECA

If you purchase an orchid that isn't already growing in LECA clay balls, you'll want to repot it before adding it to your terrarium. Remove the orchid gently from the pot in which it came and discard the bark or other medium, softly removing it from in between the roots. It may be helpful to soak the root ball in distilled water for 15 minutes to help dislodge any pieces of bark that are stuck. You can either reuse the pot it came in (after cleaning it out) or purchase a new pot. Plastic basket pots specifically made for orchids work very well and have several air holes on the bottom as well as the sides. Place the bare roots into the pot and gently fill it with rinsed LECA. Now you are ready to plant the terrarium!

Aquatic Plant Paludarium

MATERIALS

▸ Aquarium gravel from a pet store. Ask for gravel specifically for aquatic plants.

▸ Water conditioner drops to remove chlorine and heavy metals from tap water. You can also use distilled water without needing to treat it first.

▸ Large aquarium rock or driftwood. If you're using driftwood, boil it in water prior to use to remove tannins and impurities.

▸ Aquarium lamp (optional)

▸ Small air pump, tubing, and air stone (optional)

▸ Long aquarium tongs

▸ Large bowl. Make sure the bowl is made of thick glass or unbreakable acrylic; thin glass cracks easily especially when it's wet and slippery.

▸ Fishing line (optional)

▸ Scoop

▸ Paper towels

▸ A selection of aquatic and/ or semiaquatic plants (see the sidebar for some suggestions)

A paludarium is half aquarium and half terrarium. It generally has both aquatic (water-based) and terrestrial (land-based) plants inside. You can use aquatic plants with their roots immersed in water and leaves growing above water, or you can use aquatic plants that float. Paludariums can be either fully enclosed or open on top. For this project, we'll make a paludarium using a large glass fishbowl and both semi-aquatic and aquatic plants.

EASY AQUATIC PALUDARIUM PLANTS

- *Anubias* var. *nana*
- Java Fern (*Microsorum pteropus*)
- Marimo Moss Balls (*Cladophora aegagropila*)
- Red Root Floater (*Phyllanthus fluitans*)
- *Cryptocoryne* species
- Java Moss (*Taxiphyllum Barbieri*)

- Water Spangles (*Salvinia minima*)
- Duckweed (*Lemna minor*)
- Water Wisteria (*Hygrophila difformis*)
- Amazon Sword (*Echinodorus grisebachii*)
- Dwarf Water Lily (*Nymphaea stellata*)
- Banana Plant (*Nymphoides aquatica*)

Step 1: Place all materials on a sturdy surface and have paper towels handy for easy clean up. Rinse plants with room temperature tap water. Your gravel, depending on the type you choose, may also need to be rinsed. Check the manufacturer's instructions.

Step 2: Using your scoop, fill the bowl with about 3 inches (7.6 cm) of gravel. Flatten the gravel with your hand to even it out. For this project I am using a material called Eco Complete made by CaribSea.

Step 3: Next, slowly fill the bowl with water up to about 2 to 3 inches (5 to 7.6 cm) from the rim. Use either distilled water or treat tap water with conditioning drops, which remove chlorine and other harmful metals. These substances are not good for plants and can even kill animals you may be adding later.

Step 4: Place the large rock or driftwood toward the back of the bowl and gently nuzzle it down into the gravel a little. Note: I have attached an aquatic plant (*Anubias* var. *nana*) to the rock by its roots with fishing line around the rock and making a double knot at the back. This allows the plant's leaves to grow above the waterline while its roots are submerged.

Step 5: With your aquarium tongs, gently grip the base of your rooted plants and push them into the gravel at the center line of the bowl (right in front of the rock/driftwood). Since these plants grow taller, you don't want to place them at the front of the bowl.

Step 6: You can also drop in a few Marimo moss balls at this stage (rinse them first and squeeze very lightly to clean them of dirt that can get trapped inside). The moss balls can be toward the front of the bowl in the open space closest to you. If they float at first, don't worry; they will sink in a day or two.

Step 7: It's now time to add the floating plants! Make sure the leaves are facing upward and the roots are in the water. If some of them are twisted, help them out, but usually they will correct themselves in a few days. I've used Water Spangles and Red Root Floaters (my favorite!) in this set-up.

Step 8: If you'll be using an air pump to help increase the amount of air in the water, now is a good time to insert the tubing. Adding oxygen to the water keeps it from becoming cloudy and stagnant and is good for the plants (and any animals you might add to your paludarium too!). However, air pumps are not strictly necessary for this set-up. I've placed the air stone behind the rock so it won't show and detract from the view. Now is also a good time to place your paludarium where you want it to stay and set up any lighting you may have chosen to use to help plants grow more quickly and stay strong (see the Resources section). If you are not using artificial light, place the paludarium in a brightly lit location away from prolonged direct sunlight. Direct sun often causes algae to grow on the glass and heats the water up too much.

Step 9: After everything is set up and the equipment is running, add a pet (or two or three!) if you'd like. Follow any instructions from the pet store for how to acclimate your pet to its new home. See the sidebar for some great pet options.

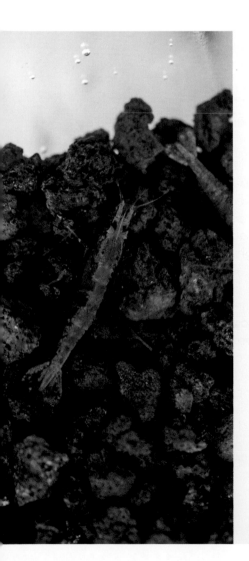

PETS FOR YOUR PALUDARIUM

There are several suitable pets you can add to your paludarium. Be sure the pet you choose will be happy and healthy living in its new home. Keep in mind that many pets will require heat or other elements you may not be able to provide with your paludarium. Here is a list of pets I recommend and their basic care requirements:

- Betta Fish: Place only one per bowl (they are also called Siamese fighting fish and will not get along with another fish of the same species). They require distilled or treated water and live happily with snails.

- Nerite Snails or Mystery Snails: These snails can be kept singly or in a group; they will not reproduce in the aquarium. Snails require distilled or treated water and this type of snail will not eat the plants. These animals are excellent at keeping a bowl clean.

- Red Cherry Shrimp (*Neocaridina heteropoda*): This dwarf freshwater shrimp can be kept with snails, as they also require distilled or treated water. Red cherry shrimp may reproduce in the aquarium. They'll also help to keep the bowl clean and will not harm plants. But don't pair cherry shrimp with fish because they are likely to become a tasty meal!

Certain animals are not suited for your paludarium, and these include goldfish, guppies, tropical fish, crabs, turtles, tadpoles, and frogs. Most of these critters either grow too big, need heated water, or can (and will!) escape this set-up.

Mini Moss Landscape

MATERIALS

- *A compressed block of coco coir*
- *Glass container with lid*
- *Moss (For this project I am using Mood Moss (Dicranum), Cushion Moss (Leucobryum), and Feather Moss (Hypnum or Ptilium. See the Resources section for sources.)*
- *Rocks in a variety of sizes*
- *Pebbles or coarse sand*
- *Long aquarium tongs*
- *Scoop*
- *Adjustable stream spray bottle filled with distilled water*
- *Paper towels*
- *Wide paintbrush*
- *Scissors*
- *Large mixing bowl*
- *Springtails (optional; see the sidebar)*

Moss is a moisture-loving miniature plant that adapts well to life in a closed terrarium. It comes in several varieties; some that look like tiny grassy hills, others that look like miniature ferns, and still others that appear to be little pine trees (see the moss profiles on page 22). For these reasons, moss is the perfect choice for creating mini landscapes like the one in this project.

Step 1: Place the compressed coco coir brick in the mixing bowl with warm water and wait about a half-hour until you can break it apart. Mix it with your hands until it looks like regular potting soil and is no longer compacted.

Step 2: Fill the bottom of the glass terrarium container with coco coir to about 2 inches (5 cm) high at the front of the jar and 4 to 5 inches (10.2 to 12.7 cm) high at the back. Pack it down with your hands and brush away any particles stuck to the glass. (Tip: if you have a spray bottle with an adjustable stream, turn it to a hard stream and spray the glass just above the soil line. This washes down any stubborn soil that doesn't want to be brushed away.) The planting material should be at a slant like a miniature hillside, tall in the back and low in the front.

Step 3: Next, place the largest rocks in the middle to upper portion of the "hill" and nestle them in slightly so they stay put. I normally use either one very large rock or 2 to 3 medium-sized rocks placed randomly. If any soil has fallen toward the front of the glass, pack it down again into place. These will be the mountains in your mini landscape scene.

4

5

6

Step 4: Now take handfuls of Mood Moss (cut off most of the brownish parts underneath with scissors if necessary; this will not harm the moss) and plant it so that the "hill" you created is covered. If the moss came as one large piece simply pull it apart or cut it with scissors. Place the pieces tightly around the rock "mountains." Leave a small gap of space at the bottom front because you will be adding other moss and stone to this area.

Step 5: Place a few randomly sized pieces of Cushion Moss at the bottom front of the bowl. Here I used small and medium pieces, ranging in size from about 1½ to 3½ inches (4 to 9 cm). The larger the jar, the bigger the pieces you can use.

Step 6: Fill in any gaps where the potting material shows through with smaller rocks and pebbles/sand. Use a mini scoop, measuring spoon, or tongs to put it in place. Then brush away any stray bits with your paintbrush.

WHAT IS THE BEST MATERIAL TO PLANT MOSS IN?

As you've already learned, moss is a very special kind of plant. It doesn't have a root system like most plants do. Instead it absorbs moisture through its leaves by taking in tiny water particles from the air. Most mosses like to grow in shady, humid environments with lots of moisture in the air. What does this have to do with choosing the best planting material for your mossarium? Well, since moss doesn't get nutrients and moisture through a root system, the main thing to look for in a planting material is water retention. If the material holds onto water, it will help keep humidity high inside the terrarium. See chapter 1 for more on growing mixes.

Step 7: To give the scene its final touches, use individual pieces of either Tree Moss, Fern Moss, or Feather Moss placed randomly to look like tiny trees or bushes. In this scene, we are using Feather Moss. With the long tongs, gently grasp the piece of moss at the base of the stem and push it down into the planting material. I usually place these pieces around the rocks where they will be most visible.

Step 8: Spray the inside of the glass one last time to remove any dirt particles, then turn the nozzle to a fine mist and spray the surface of the moss. Wipe down the inside of the glass with paper towels and place the lid on top. If you get a lot of "fog" or condensation on the glass, it's most likely because the interior of the terrarium is not the same temperature as the room. If the "fog" bothers you, simply crack the lid slightly or periodically wipe down the inner glass with a paper towel.

SPRINGTAILS

Springtails are tiny insects that live in the soil and feed on decaying plant material. They also love to eat mold or mildew, bacteria, and fungi. Because mold is a very common problem in closed terrariums, and it can quickly kill plants, springtails make a great clean-up crew! I add springtails to all my own terrariums and I never see a bit of mold. My plants are also healthier because they clean up any dead plant material. The best time to add these creatures is right after you finish planting your terrarium. Just pour them on top of the moss and they will get right to work. Read up on springtails and other beneficial insects in chapter 4 and find sources for these beneficial insects in the Resources section.

Resources

Air Plants and Bromeliads
www.airplanthub.com
www.airplantsupplyco.com
www.etsy.com/shop/MyGreenObsession
www.glassboxtropicals.com

Lithops
www.etsy.com/shop/LittleEmeraldThumb
www.microlandscapingdesign.com
www.fatandprickly.com

Praying Mantis
www.usmantis.com
www.panterrapets.com
www.mantiszoo.com

Carnivorous Plants
www.carnivorousplantnursery.com
www.californiacarnivores.com
www.curiousplant.com

Orchids
www.paphparadise.com
www.andysorchids.com
www.glassboxtropicals.com
www.orchidweb.com
www.logees.com

Bonsai Trees
www.elementalnursery.com
www.bonsaioutlet.com
www.logees.com

Tropical Terrarium Plants
www.glassboxtropicals.com
www.etsy.com/shop/MyGreenObsession
www.joshsfrogs.com
www.logees.com

Glass Containers
www.amazon.com/shop/dbterrariums
www.hobbylobby.com
www.modernvaseandgift.com
Home Goods
TJ Maxx

Marimo Moss Balls
www.aquaticarts.com
PetSmart

Aquatic Plants
www.sevenseasupply.com
www.aquaticarts.com
www.imperialtropicals.com

Cherry Shrimp/Snails
www.sevenseasupply.com
www.imperialtropicals.com

Moss
www.etsy.com/shop/eileenb58
www.amazon.com/shop/dbterrariums
www.etsy.com/shop/MossUnlimited

Beneficial Insects, Springtails, Isopods
www.glassboxtropicals.com
www.joshsfrogs.com

Feeder Insects
www.joshsfrogs.com
www.rainbowmealworms.net
www.dubiaroaches.com
Petco
PetSmart

Substrates and Soils
www.amazon.com/shop/dbterrariums
www.joshsfrogs.com/substrates.html

Fertilizers and Pest-Control Products
www.amazon.com/shop/dbterrariums
www.logees.com

Succulents and Cacti
www.thenextgardener.com
www.mountaincrestgardens.com

Artificial Lighting for Terrariums
www.sansiled.com
www.onf.com.tw/?lang=en
www.ikea.com/us/en/cat/work-lamps-20502
www.amazon.com/shop/dbterrariums

Scale Miniatures
www.woodlandscenics.com
www.preiserusa.com

Animal Figurines
www.us.schleich-s.com
www.safariltd.com

Wall Planters
www.etsy.com/shop/pupax
www.etsy.com/shop/wowsucculents
www.amazon.com/shop/dbterrariums

About the Author

Patricia Buzo is the artist, owner, and photographer behind Doodle Bird Terrariums. She started out as a stay-at-home mom with a passion for plants. After creating a terrarium for her young daughter, she was bitten by the bug and soon after began offering her creations for sale on Etsy. Over the past 12 years she has worked hard to grow her business and promote the hobby on social media, becoming a top influencer in the field. She is currently writing on the subject and creating instructional videos.

Find out more at www.DoodleBirdTerrariums.com

Acknowledgments

First and foremost, I want to thank my husband, Jose, for all your patience and support. Always allowing me to work in a quiet environment and having me distracted from family time wasn't easy, but I so very much appreciate it over these past several months. I love you with all my heart.

I'd also like to thank my colleague Ivan Danou for always being ready to answer my endless requests for opinions and carnivorous plant care tips. You are definitely an expert, and I could not have written this book without you. Also, I should probably thank you for being an enabler with all things plants.

Tracy Walsh, without your amazing photography skills this book would not have turned out so beautifully. You made photo shoots a breeze, and because I was so nervous about getting everything just right, I truly appreciate your calm. We will have a few funny stories to tell about this experience, won't we? Thank you.

To my mom, Shari, who helped me behind the scenes at each and every photo shoot (and, of course, who raised me)—thank you so much. I love you.

To my daughter, Janeli, who had to hear all my "boring plant stories;" thank you for listening.

Thank you to everyone on my publishing team at Quarto, but especially Jessica Walliser for walking

me through my first authoring experience. You were always there when I had a question or concern and to simply give me encouragement when I needed it!

And last but not least, thank you to all of the awesome kid models and their parents! The Peña family (Bruno Marcelo and Miranda), the Lopez/Mueller family (Nayeli and Marlo), the Cortez family (Gabriela), the McCastle family (Anthony), the Nistler family (Zoe and Mya), the Walsh family (Evan), the Woodstrom family (Ainsley and Evelyn), and the Andrashko-Euclide family (Hazel and Cecilia).

Index